Tales from the

TEXAS
LONGHORNS

STEVE RICHARDSON

www.SportsPublishingLLC.com

ISBN: 1-59670-047-5

Publishers: Peter L. Bannon and Joseph J. Bannon Sr.
Senior managing editor: Susan M. Moyer
Acquisitions editor: Mike Pearson
Developmental editor: Elisa Bock Laird
Art director: K. Jeffrey Higgerson
Dust jacket design: Joseph T. Brumleve
Interior layout: Dustin J. Hubbart
Imaging: Dustin J. Hubbart
Photo editor: Erin Linden-Levy
Media and promotions managers: Randy Fouts (national),
    Maurey Williamson (print)

Printed in the United States of America

Sports Publishing L.L.C.
804 North Neil Street
Champaign, IL 61820

Phone: 1-877-424-2665
Fax: 217-363-2073
www.SportsPublishingLLC.com

Covering college football has been the life for many members of the Football Writers Association of America. I became the executive director of this now-more-than 800-member FWAA in 1996. And since then, I have gained an even greater appreciation for how newspapers, magazines, the Internet, and radio and television outlets cover teams. I also believe I have a better understanding of the very important roles played by sports information directors at major schools, many of whom are also FWAA members.

I am dedicating this college football book to all those who work college football Saturdays. There is a long line of great sportswriters who have made the games college kids play during the fall come to life on the sports pages in this country. And there is a long line of great SIDs who have poured their hearts and souls into college football. Two of those, John Bianco and Bill Little of Texas (both noted in this book), have been longtime FWAA members and are among the best in the business.

The writing profession started with such luminaries as Grantland Rice, who helped formulate the FWAA All-America team, and others such as Fred Russell, Maury White, Furman Bisher, Blackie Sherrod, Edwin Pope, Sid Hartman, and many, many others. Into the 1990s and into the new millennium, some of those names have been replaced by people such as Dick Weiss, Mark Blaudschun, Ivan Maisel, Tony Barnhart, Dave Sittler, Tom Shatel, Blair Kerkhoff, Dennis Dodd, Kelly Whiteside, Wally Hall, Ron Higgins, and Mike Griffith, who are at their computers pounding out sometimes thousands of words each week on the sport of college football.

This is just a slice of those Saturdays from the state of Texas, where the Longhorns have acted out their share of tales on the field.

Steve Richardson
October 6, 2005

CONTENTS

ACKNOWLEDGMENTS

Pulling together a comprehensive collection of stories involving University of Texas football was no easy task. But it was made much easier with great cooperation from those associated with one of the most storied programs in college football.

Special thanks go to former UT coaches and players for their time spent in the development of this book. Over the years, people such as Darrell Royal, Mack Brown, Fred Akers, Frank Broyles, Barry Switzer, Greg Davis, James Street, Jimmie McDowell, John Mackovic, David McWilliams, Peter Gardere, Robert Brewer, Rooster Andrews, Eddie Phillips, Jeff Ward, Chris Simms, Roy Williams, Ted Nance, Ricky Williams, and Earl Campbell have always been generous with their time and interviews.

The Texas sports information staff of John Bianco, Scott McConnell, Brian Hernandez, and Bill Little were of great help in providing time and access to well-kept files. Ken Capps, a Dallas UT alum who lives and breathes the fortunes of the Longhorns, was of immeasurable help as well.

Charlie Fiss of the SBC Cotton Bowl opened his library of pictures and files and greatly assisted the development the book. Special thanks to Charlie for his conscientious work.

—Steve Richardson

INTRODUCTION

Longhorns football has been a staple of Texas life for about 110 years. But it wasn't until the 1940s and the reign of coach D.X. Bible that the Longhorns arrived on the national scene and began to weave their excellence into the fabric of college football history.

The Longhorns went to their first bowl game after the 1942 season and started a run of great games in the Cotton Bowl with a 14-7 victory over Georgia Tech. The 1940s signaled the rollicking era of Bobby Layne and later the coaching eras of Blair Cherry and Ed Price.

Texas football teams were competing at a high level until 1956, when the team dropped off to a 1-9 record under Price.

Then came the golden period of UT football, when coach Darrell Royal led the Longhorns to Southwest Conference dominance and undisputed national championships in 1963 and 1969. Royal turned the tide of OU dominance in the State Fair game as well and developed a program with class and dignity.

Upon Royal's retirement after the 1976 season, the Longhorns celebrated their first Heisman Trophy winner, big Earl Campbell, in 1977. Under the watchful eye of coach Fred Akers, UT also had a close brush with a national championship during 1977 and again in 1983.

The "Shock the Nation Tour" under coach David McWilliams gave UT a brief respite from football mediocrity in 1990. Then the rather inconsistent coaching tenure of John Mackovic followed. Included in that period, however, was one of the most stunning upsets in UT history, a victory over Nebraska in the first Big 12 title game.

Another Heisman Trophy winner was crowned in 1998, the season Mack Brown debuted as the UT coach, as Ricky Williams provided thrills for a new generation of Longhorns fans.

Tales from the Texas Longhorns depicts the great games, the awesome plays, and the legendary players such as Layne, Campbell, Williams, and Outland Trophy winners Scott Appleton, Tommy Nobis, and Brad Shearer.

It's a must-read for Longhorns fans everywhere!

CHAPTER ONE

The Early Years

The First UT Game

The University of Texas played its first football game in 1893 when the varsity sent a 15-to-16-man contingent to face the Dallas Football Club on Thanksgiving Day in Dallas. Undefeated and unscored upon for several years previous, the Dallas team fell to Texas 18-16 before 2,000 fans at Fairgrounds Park.

Texas played three more games that season and won them all, including another 16-0 victory over Dallas. In fact, Texas won its first 10 games of varsity competition before losing to Missouri 28-0 in the final game of the 1894 season.

First Out-of-State Game

The first Texas team to play any games outside of the state of Texas was the 1896 team, coached by Harry Robinson. During a 4-2-1 season, Texas played at Tulane on November 14 and posted a 12-4 victory in New Orleans. Two days later, Texas lost to LSU in Baton Rouge 14-0.

Texas didn't make another trip outside of the state of Texas until 1899, when it lost to Vanderbilt in Nashville. But UT's mini-road trip in 1896 was nothing compared to the Sewanee road trip of 1899, three years later.

UT Part of Sewanee History

Texas lost to Sewanee 12-0 on November 9, 1899, in the first game of an incredible 2,300-mile road trip in which the Sewanee Iron Men won five games in six days—all by shutouts.

Sewanee (Tennessee) is now a Division III school that competes in the Southern Collegiate Athletic Conference. But in those days it played a major schedule. Four of 21 players on the 1899 team were from the state of Texas. Handlers brought two barrels of Tennessee spring water. But the team manager forgot the team's new shoes at the train station in Tennessee and had to send for them. The shoes arrived in Austin right before the game.

Sewanee captain Henry "Diddy" Seibels, who scored both touchdowns in the victory over Texas, suffered a split head. It was reported in the *Austin American-Statesman* that he "bled like a hog." Seibels didn't leave the game, however, because in those days a player could not return once departed.

Texas, early in the game, drove to the Sewanee 15. But Sewanee alum Bob "Pop" Atkins stood up and yelled, "This $250 says Texas will not score in the game." He had several takers among the crowd of 2,000, and he accumulated a small fortune when Sewanee shut out Texas.

Of course, Texas fans could take solace in the fact that Sewanee beat Texas A&M 10-0 the next day in Houston. Then Sewanee beat Tulane (23-0) in New Orleans, LSU (34-0) in Baton Rouge, and Memphis (12-0) during its whirlwind trip. Sewanee compiled a 12-0 record and shut-out 11 of its opponents.

Strike up the UT Band

In 1900, UT's colors were declared to be orange and white by the Board of Regents, and the first UT band was formed.

A group of 16 UT students were organized by chemical engineering professor E.P. Schoch. They gathered in a room of Old

Main for the first rehearsal of the band, practicing with two drums and 12 other instruments, which were purchased at a pawn shop for $150.

The band's first uniforms were linen dusters (white linen overcoats) and white caps with black bills. They were bought at a downtown department store.

The band began playing for football games that season. However, women didn't join the band until World War II, when they were needed to fill the gaps created by men going off to war.

In 1928, Texas acquired the colors burnt orange and white because the bright orange jerseys had faded. That lasted a decade, until a dye shortage forced the Longhorns to go back to the bright orange.

"Eyes of Texas" Origin

In 1903, the "Eyes of Texas" was written by John Lang Sinclair, a member of the UT Band. Sinclair was requested to write a song for the university minstrel show at the old Hancock Opera House. Given only a few hours to write the song, he remembered a saying of the university's president at that time. Dr. Lamdin Prather told students to remember "the eyes of Texas are upon you."

Sinclair fitted the words into the tune "I've Been Working on the Railroad." He wrote the words on brown scrap paper while sitting in the upstairs of Old B Hall.

Sinclair wrote the song in imitation of Dr. Prather, who was rather serious and solemn in delivering the expression. Dr. Prather had been a student at Washington and Lee, where he heard school president General Robert E. Lee address the students: "Gentlemen, the eyes of the South are upon you."

A quartet, which included Jim Cannon, later an Amarillo businessman, sang the song as part of a minstrel act. He recounted the event in an article in *The Dallas Morning News* on September 6, 1931.

"Before we finished the first verse the house was in uproar, and by the time 'til Gabriel blows the horn' was reached, the audience must have been semi-hysterical, judging by their antics. They pounded the floor and shouted for an encore, which we willingly gave again and again and still again."

Soon the students joined in. And the band learned the tune and words the next day and was playing, "The Eyes of Texas Are Upon You."

Many of the students left believing it was a joke. In 1905, the song was sung at the funeral of Dr. Prather and achieved its place in UT history.

How "Longhorns" Stuck

In 1903 a *Daily Texan* sportswriter labeled the UT team "Longhorns." His name was D.A. Frank, a UT student from 1903 to 1905.

He was instructed by editor-in-chief of *The Daily Texan* Alex Weisburg, "D.A., hereafter in every sports article, call the team the Longhorns, and we'll soon have it named."

In a letter to the editor of *The Daily Texan* in 1943, Frank remembers, "I obeyed instructions. After Clint Brown's partial year, I became editor-in-chief and continued the instructions to the sportswriters. Along about 1906 or 1907, the name became official."

The Forfeit Game

In 1910, Texas won a 1-0 forfeit on November 5 in Waco when Baylor left the field at halftime with the score tied 6-6. The Baylor team had a dispute with the referee. It was the only defeat for Baylor (6-1-1) that season.

The Cactus, the UT yearbook, portrayed the Baylor game as follows.

"…The squad, accompanied by scores of rooters, went to Waco to meet Baylor. But why waste good white paper on the fiasco? Baylor decided she had a better chance of winning if she turned the game into a debate. No sooner thought than done; the officials demurred and gave the game to Varsity, 1-0."

The Death of a Coach

W.S. (Billy) Wasmund, whose credentials were playing for coach Fielding "Hurry-Up" Yost at Michigan, compiled a 6-2 record in 1910, his only full season as UT's coach.

The Cactus recounted the enthusiasm Coach Wasmund had created on the UT campus: "Everyone is rejoicing in the fact that he will be back to coach the 1911 squad, and it is a safe prediction that he will surpass the success of [1910]."

But Wasmund lasted only three games into the next season. He suffered a mysterious accident. He walked in his sleep and fell from the second story of his home a week before Texas was to play TCU. He died four days later at the age of 26.

Wasmund was replaced as UT coach by another Michigan man, David W. Allerdice, who had been an assistant coach for Yost.

Series-Ending Game

Texas and Texas A&M played as part of the No-TSU-Oh carnival (Houston spelled backward) on November 13, 1911.

Three Longhorns suffered broken bones in the game. UT students enacted a none-too-flattering parody of the Texas A&M marching unit. And after Texas's 6-0 victory, a fight broke out among opposing fans.

The Texas-Texas A&M series was halted until 1915 and then resumed on campus sites.

Rockne Pays Homage to Edmond

UT's fabled three-sport star Pete Edmond lettered in football as an end from 1913 to 1915. He lettered in basketball from 1913 to 1916 as a guard. And he lettered in baseball from 1913 to 1916 as a third baseman. In addition, during his senior year he competed in wrestling as a middleweight.

Knute Rockne played end on the Notre Dame team that defeated Texas 30-7 in 1913. He played opposite Edmond.

"I'll never forget that player as long as I live," Rockne said later. "I played football against the best teams in the East. I played against the best in the West and against the best in the other sections. But never was I forced to go up against a better wing. He was as clean as a whistle, but he played hard football. Oh, how hard did he play. And I have always admired him for it.

"That was one great star in the Southwest who did not get his just dues when All-American teams were picked," Rockne added. "I can certainly vouch for that fact. He was a terror when his team was completely overwhelmed. I have often wondered just what heights he achieved when playing against a traditional rival."

UT's Man on the Sidelines

Doc Henry Reeves—UT's manager, trainer, masseur, and doctor—died in 1915 after suffering a stroke at the Texas A&M game. The son of a freed slave, Reeves was only 44 when he died. But Doc Henry served UT athletic teams from 1895 to 1915.

He was described by—*The Longhorn* (alumni newsletter) as "the most famous character connected with football at the University of Texas." After suffering the stroke during the 13-0 loss to Texas A&M, Reeves was paralyzed for two months before dying. He received help from the student body, who took up a collection to help pay for his medical bills.

The Naming of Bevo: Take Your Pick

In 1916, UT football manager Stephen Pinckney obtained a $1 subscription from 124 alumni to purchase a steer and transport him by private car from West Texas. A presentation was held before 15,000 people assembled for the Texas A&M game won by Texas 21-7. It was the first UT-A&M game in Austin since 1909.

Pinckney was engaged in fighting Mexican rustlers along the Rio Grande after graduation and found an orange-and-white-colored steer.

So how did the mascot get his name?

One story goes this way: Texas A&M students later stole him and branded him with the 13-0 score of the previous season, which had been a big upset. The word Bevo came out of the brand, in which Texas fans turned 13 into a B, made the dash into an E and inserted the V. The 0 was already there.

The original Bevo's head was hung up inside the old UT athletic building after the steer was laid to rest. *Ronald Martinez/Getty Images*

But two other theories are possible as well.

Bevo could have become the nickname because it was the name of a soft drink of the day. Also, there's a theory that the term *beeve* is the plural of beef and was used as a term for a steer that was going to become a meal. And in those days adding an "o" to a nickname of a friend or mascot was common.

Neglected, Then Served for Dinner

With the beginning of World War I, the original Bevo was left out on the farm and forgotten. He eventually wound up on the butcher's block.

Bevo's next appearance was in the form of a meal in honor of the 1920 UT team, which upset Texas A&M 7-3 for the Southwest Conference title. The A&M captain, school president, and coaches were invited. Bevo's hide was halved. The branded side was given to the Aggies. And UT kept the other side.

Bevo I's head was hung in Z Hall, a building that housed the athletic department at the time. In 1928, after a pregame rally, some SMU students stole the head, and SMU won the next day 6-2. The head was recovered and put in old Gregory Gym until 1943, when Aggies fans dehorned him.

Another Bevo appeared in 1932. But the mascot wasn't a fixture at UT games until 1966. Handled by the Silver Spurs, a men's honorary organization, the steers are loaned to the University by the state of Texas with the understanding that they will be retired after a reasonable period of time. Bevo's horns commonly span six feet from tip to tip.

UT's Other Mascot

Pig, a tan and white pit bull mix, was adopted as UT's mascot before Bevo became popular. Pig was brought to Austin when he was seven weeks old by L. Theo Bellmont, the school's athletic director at the time. He was named for Gus "Pig" Dittmar, a center on the UT football team who was said to slip through the defensive line like a greased pig.

During a game in 1914, the athlete and dog were standing side by side on the sideline. It was noticed that both were bow-legged. Hence, the dog had a name.

Pig died in 1923 after he was hit by a Model T at the corner of 24th and Guadalupe streets. He lay in state in front of the Co-Op in a casket draped with orange and white ribbon before he was buried under a small grove of oak trees near the old law building. A marker was laid on the grave with the epitaph: "Pig's Dead Dog Gone." A re-creation of the original tombstone was laid there in the spring of 2001.

Perfect Ending

In 1919, coach Dana X. Bible's Aggies beat Texas 7-0, capping a perfect season in which Texas A&M did not allow a point. Bible, after a stint at Nebraska, wound up coaching at Texas as well.

It was the third straight time UT had gone to College Station and not even scored a point, losing 13-0 in 1915 and 7-0 in 1917. It was the last game for UT coach Bill Juneau after three seasons.

The Cactus reported the game was played "in a cold norther, with a light drizzle at times. The Farmers played the wind with punts and drove to the Longhorn 10. They scored early in the second quarter. UT advanced to the A&M five in the third quarter, but was held on downs."

1920 Battle of Unbeatens

A year later in Austin, Texas won the Southwest Conference title by registering a very important 7-3 victory over the Aggies in a battle of unbeaten teams. UT wound up giving up only one touchdown and a total of 13 points during the 1920 season.

The Longhorns, Aggies, and Arkansas were unbeaten in SWC play going into the game (Arkansas had played neither school). Arkansas fell out of first with a tie to Rice on that same Thanksgiving Day.

Francisco Domingues scored Texas's touchdown. *The Cactus* reported: "Domingues, it was asserted, had been saved by the coach for two or three games for the expressed purpose of training for the A&M game. The coach had worked him extra hard on dummies, speed and plunging. His massive shoulders gave him a driving power that resulted in his being able to hit the line with such a force that opponents would be thrust from side to side while some would be hanging on for a free ride. It was almost impossible to stop him."

Bible's Alamo Story

In 1922, the Texas-Texas A&M game was tied in Austin. In the history of the SWC at that point, no Aggies team had been able to beat Texas in Austin.

Bible remembered that in defense of the Alamo Lieutenant Colonel William B. Travis drew a line with his sword along the dirt floor and invited all who wanted to stay to step over the line. Legend has it that all stepped over except Jim Bowie, who was unable to walk and was pulled over in his cot.

"Those who want to go out and be known as the members of an A&M team that defeated Texas in Austin, step over the line," Bible said. He was stampeded by the rush. The Aggies beat Texas 14-7.

Making a National Statement

In October, 1923 Texas beat powerful Vanderbilt 16-0 in Dallas behind back Oscar Eckhardt, who was described in *The Longhorn T,* a monthly newsletter published by the UT Athletics Council, as follows:

"...Taking many hard knocks, but at the end of the game, the big Texas half was going as strong as ever." The article went on to say, "[Ed] Stewart the Texas coach does not coddle his players. He puts them through the toughest sort of scrimmage sessions, and when the big games come they have thus far been able to stand the 'gaff.'"

Blinky Horn, a Nashville sportswriter, wrote: "In Texas, Oscar Eckhardt has displaced Davy Crockett, Sam Houston, and the Alamo. If there are any more institutions in the new country, he has set them aside."

Texas won its first six games that season by outscoring its opponents 202-0. Baylor tied the Longhorns 7-7 in the next game. UT won its last two games, 26-14 over Oklahoma and 6-0 over Texas A&M, to finish 8-0-1.

After the Vanderbilt victory, Florida offered to play a postseason game against the Longhorns in Jacksonville, Florida, during the week following Thanksgiving. SWC rules and a Texas faculty rule forbade Texas from taking Florida up on the offer. But it was an indication that Texas had reached the big time of college football, because Florida was considered one of the strongest teams in the country.

Boardroom Title

SMU won its first Southwest Conference title in 1923 but did not play Texas that season. Baylor tied Texas to drop the Longhorns into second place. SMU was awarded the title because it was undefeated and untied.

A decision was made to award the SWC title to SMU during a conference meeting at the old Oriental Hotel in Dallas. Texas fans were furious about the decision and dubbed SMU the "Oriental Hotel Champions." The next season, however, SMU defeated Texas 10-6.

Moving to Memorial Stadium

After leaving its previous football home, Clark Field, Texas lost to Baylor 28-10 in its first game at Memorial Stadium on November 8, 1924. But the vision and dreams of UT athletic director L. Theo Bellmont had been realized.

Texas's new home seated 27,000 fans and was dedicated before 33,000 fans three weeks later when UT defeated Texas A&M 7-0 on Thanksgiving Day. Temporary bleachers accommodated the overflow crowd.

Much to the delight of the UT fans, "Stookie" Allen caught a pass from Maurice Stallter that had been batted into the air by two Aggies backs. He ran 30 yards after the catch for a 50-yard play late in the game.

The Longhorn T reported: "No Texas team ever fought more gallantly than the Longhorns. It seemed as though the spirits of Louie Jordan and Pete Edmond, immortal Varsity grid heroes of other days who fell on the battlefields of France, inspired the Texas players with the feeling that the stadium built as a monument to Texas soldiers must be dedicated with a victory."

The stadium, at the bequest of the student body, was dedicated to the nearly 200,000 Texans (5,280 died) who fought in World War I.

More than 3,500 students and faculty members, along with the aid of Mr. and Mrs. Lutcher Stark, pledged $165,357.47 "as a guarantee that Texas will have the first stadium in the entire South and one of the best in the country."

Donations also were accepted for the stadium, which was slated to seat 50,000 fans when completed with its horseshoe. The original cost of the 27,000-seat stadium was $275,000, with East and West stands.

Shutouts Galore

From the end of the 1928 season until midway through the 1930 season, UT's defense registered 14 shutouts in 16 games. The defense was built by coach Clyde Littlefield.

In fact, UT posted 10 straight shutouts starting with a 6-0 blanking of Baylor on November 5, 1928, and ending a little more than a year later on November 16, 1929, with a 15-12 loss to TCU. That's the longest consecutive shutout streak in UT history, and it's doubtful it will ever be broken by another Texas team, given the higher-scoring offenses of modern-day football.

As a sign of the times, UT registered shutouts against 49 of 89 opponents in the decade of the 1920s, for 55.1 percent.

Harrison: The Hard Hitter

In 1930 sophomore Harrison Stafford made a jarring hit on OU's Guy Warren during the second half of a 17-7 UT victory. Stafford probably suffered a concussion in the game, as his teammates had to direct him the rest of the game.

Stafford later said he couldn't remember what had happened or how he had gotten hurt.

During the same season, during a 14-0 loss to TCU, Stafford surprised the Horned Frogs' great star, Johnny Vaught, later Ole Miss's coach, on a punt return play.

"I was on the opposite side of the field," Stafford recalled years later. "Johnny Vaught didn't see me."

An account in the (Fort Worth) *Star-Telegram* recounted: "Vaught went down as though shot, his headgear jumping half off his head."

Said Mike Karow, an assistant coach at UT, years later in the *San Antonio Express:* "Staff has become such a legend because of his blocking that too many people have forgotten what a great defensive player he was. But I know we had one rule when the other team had the ball close to the sideline. The instructions were that the ends and others were to take out the interference and leave the ball carrier to Staff. There never was a finer tackler in the open field. No matter how fancy the runner was, Staff timed himself perfectly every time and knocked the daylights out of them."

Upsetting Notre Dame

During a 1934 game against Texas Tech, a week before UT was scheduled to play Notre Dame, Texas head football coach Jack Chevigny decided to attempt to trick Notre Dame scouts. Chevigny told UT halfback Bohn Hilliard to fake an injury if UT got the lead.

Sure enough, Hilliard put UT ahead by the winning score 12-6 with a long run. As he crossed the goal line, Hilliard grabbed his ankle and started yelling. He called for Jack Gray to help him off the field.

Gray, who had provided the last block on the winning score, stopped and said, "Carry you off? Hell, I ran as far as you did."

The next week, Texas indeed upset Notre Dame 7-6 in South Bend. It was Notre Dame's first season-opening loss in 38 years. And it was Hilliard who provided all the points Texas would need early in the game.

Gray recovered an Irish fumble on the opening kickoff. Four plays later, Hilliard ran eight yards for the touchdown and then added the extra point.

The flamboyant Chevigny beat his alma mater, Notre Dame, in clearly his biggest victory during his three-year tenure in Austin.

Eye on Wolfe

Hugh Wolfe wound up being the first UT player taken in the NFL draft in 1938 (second round by the Pittsburgh Steelers). Wolfe's selection has started a string of 68 straight drafts (through the 2005 draft) in which Texas has had at least one player selected. UT had no players selected in the first two drafts.

Wolfe arrived at Texas almost totally blind in one eye and had poor eyesight in the other. He had measles when he was three. His nicknames were "Big Bad Wolfe" as a freshman and later "Blind Tom."

Wolfe did not play in 1935 after recovering from an eye operation. In 1936, Texas tied LSU 6-6 in the opener. On one run, Wolfe, still suffering from poor eyesight, became confused and ran in the wrong direction. Wolfe recalled in 1962 in the (Fort Worth)

Star-Telegram that his roommate Red Atchison screamed at him, "'This way, Blind Tom!' He straightened me out."

Later that season Hugh Wolfe's 95-yard kickoff return versus No. 2-ranked Minnesota was one of the few bright spots in the Longhorns' 47-19 loss to the Golden Gophers, who went on to win the national championship.

The 95-yard kickoff return was a UT record at the time and was not broken for 42 years. Johnny "Lam" Jones returned a kickoff 100 yards against SMU in 1978.

"The kickoff return was a fluke," Wolfe said. "I picked out the biggest one and ran straight at him, faked left, cut right to see nothing but daylight and the man who held the ball for the kick. He was just getting to his feet when I said, 'Goodbye.' Shirley Temple could have made that TD."

Chevigny's Strategy

UT coach Frank Chevigny (1934-1936) had a strategy of taking his starters out of the game after they had built leads.

In a 1936 game against Baylor, the Longhorns had built an 18-0 lead going into the fourth quarter. Chevigny, as was his custom, took his starters out and sent them to the showers.

But by the time they could get out of the showers and back out on the field, Baylor had rallied for a 21-18 defeat of the Longhorns by scoring three times.

Chevigny resigned after the 1936 season with a 13-14-2 overall record and through the 2004 season still stands as the only UT coach to post a losing career record at the school.

CHAPTER TWO

Moving into the Big Time

The Hiring of Bible

The University of Texas, tired of the lackluster 1935 and 1936 seasons under coach Jack Chevigny, opened up the bank vault to get a new coach in 1937.

Dana X. Bible, who had fashioned successful coaching tenures at Texas A&M and Nebraska, was hired for $15,000, $3,000 more than he was earning as a coach at Lincoln.

UT officials raised the president's salary to $17,500 so he would be making more than Bible. Bible signed a 10-year contract that would pay him $7,500 as football coach and $7,500 as athletic director annually.

Bible was welcomed to Austin with a large parade. One float had the words "Bible: The Answer to Prayer" inscribed in Old English script on the side.

Money Behind the Hire

H.L. Lutcher Stark, a millionaire who owned a half-million acres in Texas and Louisiana, was responsible for luring Bible to Texas.

"Just what part, Mr. Stark, would you expect to have in athletics at Texas?" Bible asked at the time of his hiring.

"Just sitting on the sidelines," Stark said.

"What if I put you off the sidelines?" Bible asked.

"Well," Stark said, "I've been put off by worse coaches than you, D.X."

"A lot of people will be involved in our program," Bible said. "And none can be given special privileges."

"Then I'll just buy the best seats I can," Stark said. "And when you need help, holler."

The Bible Plan

D.X. Bible had a plan. But it took time to implement. Bible's first UT team in 1937 was 2-6-1, and his second team in 1938 was 1-8. Those first two seasons his teams were nicknamed, "Ali Bible and His Forty Sieves."

Bible tried to change the "pay-for-play scheme" in college athletics.

"When a boy is contacted and invited, he is told he will receive the benefits of being a member of the team only so long as he is eligible scholastically," Bible said. "But so long as he remains eligible, and in school, these benefits continue until graduation regardless of whether he is able to make the team, or is injured and cannot compete for the remainder of his college career."

As part of his plan, Bible asked alumni to report on the academic and athletic prowess of high school athletes in their areas. The state of Texas was divided into districts. And alumni were assigned responsibilities for recruiting good high school players.

The five-foot-eight Bible was extremely organized and proper. During games he always wore a starched white dress shirt and tie. He usually just sat on the bench.

"D.X. [Dana Xenophon] Bible was a coach everybody could respect," said Malcolm Kutner, UT's first All-American. "You could look up to him kind of like you did your preacher. I never heard him use a curse word other than damn."

D.X. Bible was the coach who put UT on the college football map.
Cotton Bowl Athletic Association

Lighting the Tower

Coinciding with Bible's first season in 1937, UT began lighting its 27-story UT Tower in orange and white lights when the team won.

It was first lit for a football event on November 6, 1937, following a 9-6 victory over Baylor.

Hugh Wolfe was a hero after kicking a 36-yard field goal from a poor angle to beat the fourth-ranked Bears. UT quarterback Henry Mintermayer told Wolfe, who was almost totally blind in one eye, that he couldn't even see the goalposts. But Wolfe talked his way onto the field and kicked the game winner.

UT lost 10 straight games before the tower was lit again for a football victory, a 7-6 win over Texas A&M in the final game of the 1938 season.

Eventually victory lights were displayed for athletic victories other than football. The tower still is lit in all orange for football victories over Texas A&M. The tower shaft is white and observation and column decks are orange for other football victories.

Block That Kick

Before the 7-6 upset of Texas A&M, Texas had lost its first eight games of the 1938 season. Included in that streak was a loss the previous week to No. 1-ranked TCU 28-6. And UT's winless streak nearly kept going.

Holding a 7-0 lead, Texas tried a reverse in the final minute of the game and fumbled. Texas A&M recovered the fumble and scored to narrow the score to 7-6.

Texas A&M's Dick Todd set up to kick the extra point. But UT's Ted Dawson got Roy Baines to mount his back and block the kick.

"The next day I was down in Brenham on a recruiting trip," UT line coach Bully Gilstrap told the *Austin American-Statesman*. "And one of the Aggies there said, 'You've got one of the tallest football players I ever saw there in my life.'"

Energizing Victory

A last-second 14-13 victory in 1939 over Arkansas energized the UT program. With Texas trailing Arkansas 13-7 with under a minute remaining in the game, Bible sent a message to the Longhorn Band to play "The Eyes of Texas."

During the song, the Longhorns went into formation, and halfback R.B. Patrick completed a short pass to Jack Crain, who caught the ball over his shoulder and reversed field for a 71-yard touchdown. With the score tied at 13-13, Crain kicked the winning point. UT had won its first SWC opener since 1933.

"That play and that victory changed our outlook, mine, the players', the student body's and the ex-students'," Bible said. "Things had been going pretty badly up until that game. The way was still long, but we had tasted the fruits of victory and we were on our way."

The Longhorns would finish 5-4 that season, marking their first winning record in five seasons.

"That was the turning point for Texas football," Malcolm Kutner said.

"Usually we would get beat every week and the student body didn't pay any attention to you."

"Impossible Catch" Game

Texas beat Texas A&M 7-0 in 1940, snapping a 19-game Aggies winning streak. UT's victory kept the Aggies from going to the Rose Bowl and prevented them from claiming a second straight national title.

Texas A&M already had chartered a bus to Pasadena in anticipation of playing in the Rose Bowl.

It took one play to change those plans, a play called "The Impossible Catch."

Noble Doss's 35-yard, over-the-shoulder pass reception on the third play of the game set up a one-yard Pete Layden run for the only score of the game. Doss also intercepted three passes in the game, including one inside the UT 10.

"[The Impossible Catch] happened during the first 45 seconds of the game," Doss told *Longhorns Illustrated* in 1985. "I went about five yards and cut to the sideline, then cut upfield. John Kimbrough was covering me, and I gained a step or two on him when I made my last cut. Pete Layden just dropped the ball in there perfectly for me, and I went out of bounds about the one-yard line."

An incomparable picture of the catch captures Doss, in his leather helmet, with his head thrown back and his eyes closed.

The Daily Texan described the game the next day: "For Texas, it was easily the greatest victory that the orange and white has taken in 47 years of this game called football. It opened wide the pages of athletic immortality to inscribe 13 names that will bring thrills for years to come."

1941: Honors Season

As war drums beat over the Pacific and in Europe, Texas football hit new heights during the 1941 season.

Quarterback Jack Crain, also a kicker, became the first Longhorn to finish in the top 10 in the Heisman Trophy voting (10th in 1941). He was one of four Longhorns—end Malcolm Kutner, guard Chal Daniel, and back Pete Layden were the others—that season to make all-Southwest Conference.

Kutner lettered three years in football, three years in basketball and one year in track. The 170-pound Layden, with "getaway speed and surprising power for a little man," was a key to the team. He was also a passer and punter. Daniel, a ferocious blocker, was later killed in a plane crash during World War II.

Rising to No. 1, Then Falling

In 1941, UT, after rising to its first No. 1 ranking, suffered a tie and loss on opponents' late-game passes. Baylor secured a 7-7 tie with 18 seconds remaining, and TCU won 14-7 on a pass with under 10 seconds remaining.

Top-ranked Texas sported a 6-0 record when it rolled into Waco. But end Malcolm Kutner was out with an injury, and two other UT stars, back Pete Layden and quarterback Jack Crain, were nursing injuries as well.

On the short train trip back to Austin from Waco after the game, the Longhorns were served huge steaks, but few players ate their meals because they were so distraught. A crowd of 15,000 people greeted the team at the train station. The next week, TCU knocked the Longhorns out of the SWC title race.

1941 Red Candles Game Starts Another Tradition

So Texas, having dropped to a No. 10 ranking nationally after the tie and loss, was desperately searching for some good luck going into its next game at No. 2-ranked Texas A&M.

An Austin fortune teller named Madame Hipple, in accordance with a Chinese prophecy, told a group of UT coeds that red-candle burning would end an 18-year UT jinx against Texas A&M in College Station. The Longhorns had not beaten the Aggies in College Station since 1923.

In hopes of a UT victory, students began burning candles.

The legend of red candles did not raise itself again until 1950 when UT played SMU, which was ranked No. 1 in the country. UT won that game 23-20.

In 1953, the call for candles came yet again when UT was facing a powerhouse Baylor team contending for the national title. A blocked extra point was the difference in a 21-20 UT victory.

Years later, in the early 1980s, UT sports information director Bill Little called an aging Mrs. Hipple, then 85, and quoted her in a story.

"The most important person from the cradle to the grave is that person who is within you," Mrs. Hipple said. " The boys were struggling so ... they only needed something to relax the child that is within us all."

A Rose Bowl in Austin?

After the 1941 victory over Texas A&M, UT zoomed to a No. 4 national ranking with one home game remaining against Oregon on December 6, the day before Pearl Harbor.

The Rose Bowl was eyeing UT as a possible opponent for Oregon State. But the Beavers had only beaten Oregon 12-7. The Rose Bowl wanted UT to cancel its meeting with Oregon for fear of the Longhorns losing to the Ducks and spoiling an Oregon State-Texas meeting in Pasadena.

Texas coach D.X. Bible refused to cancel the Oregon game, because it would be unethical to break the contract. Plus, 20,000 servicemen were going to attend the game.

The Sugar Bowl also wanted Texas, but didn't call back when it was put on hold while Texas was dealing with the Rose Bowl. Bible talked the players out of accepting an Orange Bowl bid.

The Rose Bowl selected Duke to play Oregon State. And Texas took out its frustrations with a 71-7 victory over Oregon in Austin.

If Texas had accepted the conditional Rose bid, if would have wound up hosting the game in Austin. The Rose Bowl game was moved from the West Coast to Durham, North Carolina, because of the possibility of an invasion by the Japanese following Pearl Harbor.

UT wound up not going to a bowl after the 1941 season despite finishing fourth in the AP poll (its highest final ranking at that point) behind Minnesota, Duke, and Notre Dame. But as a consolation prize, the team was featured on the cover of *Life* magazine. Thirteen players from the 1941 Longhorns team later played professional football.

The Incomparable Rooster

Rooster Andrews was just under five feet and weighed 130 pounds when he went to Texas in 1941. Andrews, from Dallas's Woodrow Wilson High School, was part of the UT football support staff in the early to mid-1940s as a manager.

Woodrow Wilson star Malcolm Kutner asked UT coach D.X. Bible if Rooster could be an assistant manager for the Longhorns. Rooster needed another job to make ends meet. Bible found him one and lured him away from Texas A&M.

One of Texas's most colorful and enduring characters was about to spice up the UT sidelines.

"I really wanted to come here because Malcolm Kutner and I had been at Woodrow Wilson High School together," said Andrews, who stayed in Austin and made a career with a sporting goods business. "But Mr. Bible didn't have a job, and I had to have a job. I was leaving Wednesday morning and going to A&M. Kutner called me Tuesday night and told me Mr. Bible had come up with a job. It paid me $16 a month. My mother said she could send me $10 a month. So that could get me by."

Getting His Nickname

Rooster Andrews picked up his nickname shortly after he arrived at UT. He was asleep in the dormitory one night when he was summoned to go with Jack Crain and Malcolm Kutner, UT stars of the era. They wanted Andrews to climb a tree and catch a rooster named Elmer. They were going to enter Elmer in the cockfights that night.

"They gave me a flashlight," Andrews said.

"And I climbed the tree. I got up there and shone the light on Elmer."

"I asked, 'This the one, Kutner?'"

"He said, 'That's the one.'"

"I grabbed Elmer by the leg. He started clawing and cutting me. Elmer and I fell from the top of the tree and hit like a big ol' sack of cement. I held on to him."

Kutner and Crain left the freshman in an injured state. Andrews woke up the next morning with a broken arm.

"After that my name was Rooster," Andrews said.

Becoming a Kicker

Texas was having problems at kicker during the 1943 season. And Rooster had been practicing drop-kicking extra points.

"So Mr. Bible decided he would have a kicking contest and the winner would play in the next ball game," Andrews recalled. "So I won the contest."

That Saturday when the score mounted against Texas Christian, Andrews got his chance during UT's 46-7 victory over TCU.

"Our running back asked Mr. Bible, 'Why don't you let Rooster go in?' So I went in and drop-kicked a couple of extra points. That made Dutch Meyer, the TCU coach, madder than a hornet that Mr. Bible had sent the water boy in to kick extra points."

Hearing that Meyer was mad, Andrews did a very unusual thing.

"I picked up the phone and called Coach Meyer," Rooster said. "I told him the whole thing. I said, 'Don't blame Mr. Bible. If you are going to jump on anybody, jump on me.'"

"He said, 'I accept your apology.'"

Meyer, however, dared Bible to use Andrews in a much tougher game against Texas A&M 12 days later. Bible used Andrews as a kicker again, and UT won that game 27-13.

Recruiting Bobby Layne

Texas tied military team Randolph Field 7-7 in the Cotton Bowl January 1, 1944. There were no buses running because of the war. So UT coach D.X. Bible had Texas Exes transporting players in Dallas by car for practices, events, and the game.

Bobby Layne, then a high school sports star at Highland Park, was driving one of the cars. Rooster was riding in the same car and struck up a friendship with Layne.

"So when we recruited him, Mr. Bible put me on him," Rooster recalled. "When we went to the Snack Shack [on Layne's recruiting trip to Austin] I said, 'Bobby, what do you want to drink?' He looked around and said Dr. Pepper. So I ordered him a Dr. Pepper. There were two other guys with us, who Bobby didn't trust. They left, and I asked, 'Now, do you want a cold beer?'

"And he said, 'You are damn right. I thought those guys were never going to leave.'"

UT's Lure to Layne: Baseball

Bobby Layne came to Texas because of the Longhorns' strong baseball program. Layne finished with a career 28-0 record pitching against Southwest Conference teams and 39-7 overall. Five of those defeats came his freshman year.

"Bobby was a hell of a basketball player, baseball pitcher, and football player," Rooster Andrews said. "He didn't have time to do anything else. Uncle Billy [Disch] got a little bit upset when he found out Layne was going to play football. You didn't do that at the university. Bobby said I will be glad to pitch if you can work out the schedule. I can do both."

Tittle Bolts from Austin

Quarterback Y.A. Tittle from Marshall, Texas, went to UT as a freshman in 1944 and very briefly roomed with Layne and Andrews.

Andrews said an LSU assistant coach told Tittle he would never start at Texas because Layne was too good. Tittle stayed at Texas for about only 10 days and left without telling anyone. He later made All-American at LSU and was All-Pro with the New York Giants.

"Tittle had moved in with Bobby and me," Andrews said. "Mr. Bible called me one day and said, 'Have you seen Y.A? We haven't seen him. See if you could find him.'"

Tittle was already on the way to Baton Rouge.

Playing Hurt

During his freshman season of 1944, Layne played tailback in Bible's single-wingback and double-wingback offenses. However, he was not particularly suited for that offense.

That UT team finished with only a 5-4 record. But Layne was courageous in a 7-6 loss to TCU. Playing with a knee injury all season, Layne was noticeably limping against the Horned Frogs. He completed a 43-yard desperation pass late in the game, but the conversion was no good. UT could have won the SWC title with a tie.

"The only way to evaluate Layne is to say he was electric," UT coach D.X. Bible said.

The Backfield That Wasn't

UT quarterback Bobby Layne enrolled in the Merchant Marines following the 1944 season. The legendary Doak Walker, fresh out of Highland Park High School, joined his high school teammate in the adventure.

"Bobby called when they got out of the Merchant Marines and asked, 'Do we have room for Doak in our room?'" Andrews recalled.

"I said, 'Well, sure.' After I hung up, I went to Mr. Bible. I asked, 'Coach, can I have $1.50 to go the Army-Navy store to buy a cot for Doak?'"

Andrews purchased the cot, but Walker didn't become a Longhorn.

Both planned to return to Texas the following fall. Layne would return for his sophomore season. Walker was also coming to Austin to enroll as a freshman in 1945.

What a backfield that could have been. But Andrews said SMU found out that the local Dallas product was being wooed by the Longhorns. Andrews said SMU coach Matty Bell went to Walker's parents, who encouraged Walker to get off the train and spend the night in Dallas before heading to Austin. The SMU coaches intervened. And Walker never made it to Austin.

He became a Mustang and later went on to win the Heisman Trophy in 1948 as a junior at SMU.

Bechtol: Layne's Favorite Target

Hub Bechtol, a defensive and offensive end, played at Texas Tech during World War II but was lured to Texas by Bible and assistant coach Blair Cherry. Returning servicemen were allowed to change schools without losing a year of eligibility. Eventually Bechtol became the first UT player to earn All-America honors three straight seasons (1944-1946).

In the first game of the 1945 season, Texas played the military team Bergstrom Field and won 13-7. But Bechtol was ejected for fighting with tackle Dick Shellogg, a former Notre Dame player.

"We wore leather helmets with no face guards," Bechtol said. "So there were a lot of broken noses. I broke mine two or three times.

"Bobby Layne made me an All-American," Bechtol told *Orange Power Magazine*. "If you're the favorite receiver of a man like that, you get a lot of passes thrown your way. He had his favorite plays, and three of our touchdown [pass] patterns went to me. With Bobby, it was like they say: 'He never lost a game; time just ran out.'"

Walker Thwarts Trick Play

In 1945, Texas beat SMU 12-7 on November 3. Doak Walker, playing defensive back, thwarted the trick extra-point play Andrews and Layne had concocted the year before. That was the first game the players played after returning from the Merchant Marines.

"Doak used to come down there and spend weekends with us," Rooster said. "We had bragged about that play, the drop kick. So when we played SMU in '45, I went out there and we were going to pull our play. I said, 'Bobby, Doak is over there at left half. Let me make sure he is still over there.' He was. I stuck my head down.

Bobby Layne was one of UT's most colorful players on and off the field.
Cotton Bowl Athletic Association

When we came out, Doak had switched [to the other side]. So I threw the ball up in the stands. He was all primed for it."

One-Handed Joe

In the mid-1940s, Joe Mitchell, a UT lineman, was playing with a handicap. He was minus his left hand, but still blocking for UT quarterback Bobby Layne.

"[Mitchell] was from Corpus Christi," Rooster Andrews said.

"I will tell you he was as strong as anyone we had on the ball club. With that nub of his, he could paralyze you. He could get it in your rib cage and could leave you breathless. He was tough. He was strong."

Change of Coaches

D.X. Bible, after compiling a 63-31-3 record at UT and putting the Longhorns on the map nationally, retired from coaching after the 1946 season. He was the third winningest coach (198-72-3) of all time in college football when he retired.

In Bible's final season, UT posted an 8-2 record and won its first five games by a 212-19 margin before dropping games to Rice and TCU. UT finished third in the SWC behind co-champions Rice and Arkansas.

UT quarterback Bobby Layne led the team in rushing, passing, and scoring that season.

Layne's Last Requests

In 1986, hours after Texas lost to Texas A&M 16-3 in what turned out to be Fred Akers's final game as head coach, Rooster flew to Lubbock. Layne was on his deathbed. Rooster recounts that Layne, who had tubes running in and out of his nose and mouth, could only gesture.

Layne gestured to ask if Texas had won Andrews answered, "No.

"He still looked troubled, and then I said, 'You want to know if Fred lost his job?' He reared back and closed his eyes and I said, 'Yes.' He just laid back and went to sleep."

Transition Years

The post-Dana Bible era had a smooth transition initially as D.X. Bible's assistant, Blair Cherry, took over as coach. Cherry had been a successful high school coach in Amarillo before becoming a Texas assistant for Bible in 1937.

Cherry had one major thing going for him in 1947: Bobby Layne was back for his senior season. Still, change was in the air as college football was moving into the post-World War II era, and the Texas football program was transforming itself as well.

Cherry's first season as UT's head coach also ushered in air transportation at the school. Texas's players flew for the first time to a game at Oregon and won 38-13 in a Bobby Layne versus Norm Van Brocklin matchup at quarterback.

Changing the Offense

Cherry converted Layne to a T-formation quarterback for the 1947 season after getting his approval. He took Layne by car to the Chicago Cardinals and Bears camps to study the new offenses the teams were using.

Ed Price, a UT assistant coach who would eventually succeed Cherry as head coach in 1951, helped Layne make the conversion to quarterback from tailback. Layne would become UT's first four-time All-Southwest Conference selection that season.

Texas finished the 1947 season with a 10-1 record, its only loss coming against SMU 14-13, when Layne directed a fourth-quarter rally. But a missed point-after-touchdown was the difference. Texas, finishing second in the Southwest Conference, beat Alabama in the Sugar Bowl 27-7.

Look, Ma, No Pants

In a 21-6 win over Arkansas in Memphis during the 1947 season, UT tackle Ed Kelly lost his pants in the game during a rainstorm.

"Ed was wearing slicker pants that since have gone out of style," UT trainer Frank Medina told the *Houston Post.* "Somebody grabbed him and down they went. We had to rush out with blankets and change pants."

Landry as a Longhorn

During the 1947 and 1948 seasons, Cherry also had the helping hand of another Texas legend, Tom Landry. Landry, who later would coach the Dallas Cowboys, was an All-Regional fullback at Mission (Texas) High School before enrolling at Texas. Following one semester, he joined the Air Corps and flew 30 B-17 missions with the Eighth Air Force in World War II.

In November 1945, he was discharged as a first lieutenant and returned to Texas. He lettered in 1947 and 1948 as a fullback and defensive back. He was a co-captain as a senior in 1948.

In the 1949 Orange Bowl (1948 season) against Georgia, his final game at Texas, Landry gained 119 yards on 17 carries. He was particularly effective up the middle on the winning drive of a 41-28 UT victory. Landry was a big back in those days at six feet and 195 pounds.

"Tom Landry lived next door to me in the dorm. I remember Tom when he came back from the war," Rooster Andrews said. "As a freshman there were so many recruits at the time, nobody got their fair shake. He stayed hurt. He was hurt a lot. But he and Dick Harris were co-captains in 1948."

Horse Sickness

Shortly after he became coach, Cherry was informed that future star Bud McFadin, just a freshman, was homesick for the country. The big guard was bred and born in Iraan, Texas.

"What's he homesick about, his girl or his family or what?" Cherry asked.

McFadin missed his horse. So McFadin's horse was shipped to Austin his sophomore year and Bud was happy. McFadin later was a two-time All-Southwest Conference selection in 1949 and 1950 and the latter year was a consensus All-American.

Life Without Layne

UT coach Blair Cherry had to replace Layne in 1948, but the team still finished second in the Southwest Conference and wound up going to the Orange Bowl to play No. 8 Georgia.

Cherry played Paul Campbell at quarterback that season. Campbell was no Layne, but who could have been?

A prominent South Texas attorney criticized Cherry for using Campbell. When Cherry reminded him that it was difficult to replace Layne, the attorney replied: "I didn't think Layne was so hot, either."

Before the Orange Bowl game in Miami, Cherry received a letter from a group of Texas Exes: "Boy, you are on the spot ... you had better win this one or else."

With a 6-3-1 record, the Longhorns were considered a "third-rate team." Georgia had lost only one regular-season game and was an offensive juggernaut that won coach Wally Butts's third Southeastern Conference title.

In the *Miami Herald* before the game, writer Jimmy Burns used the "third-rate team" line. Burns was a friend of Georgia coach Wally Butts, and Butts was irritated that Burns had given UT some pregame motivation.

Cherry had another motivational tool he used with his team. In a pregame pep talk, Cherry pointed out that Georgia had numerous out-of-state players from the North. Cherry read the ethnic names of Georgia players and their hometowns, which dotted many northern cities.

"Look, men, it's Texas against the world!" Cherry pleaded with his underdog team, which went on to win the game 41-28.

Pregame Change-up

There was an odd part about the 1949 Orange Bowl game. The pregame ritual of warming up in the stadium went by the wayside for Texas. Because the pregame show was lengthy, Orange Bowl officials asked both teams to warm up early and then stand around and wait during the show.

Cherry, not wanting his team to cool down, would have nothing of that. He took his team to a nearby baseball field, where it warmed up before going out and beating the favored Bulldogs.

Trouble, Then Redemption

Cherry's 1949 team lost four games by a total of 10 points, finished with a 6-4 record, and did not go to a bowl game. Part of the problem was the graduation of the team's best short-yardage back. Failure to convert in short-yardage situations cost the Longhorns two of the close games.

Cherry received calls at home from irate Longhorns fans between 2:30 and 3:30 a.m. on Sundays during the season after a 20-14 loss to No. 3 Oklahoma, a 17-15 loss to No. 9 Rice, a 7-6 loss to No. 11 SMU, and a 14-13 loss to unranked TCU.

With that experience behind him, Cherry, in the following season of 1950, made the decision to leave football after the team upset No. 1-ranked SMU 23-20 in midseason in Austin. Before the game, a funeral wreath was delivered to his home. "Rest in Peace" was written on the wreath. Cherry's wife and friends tore it up and wore the flowers to the game.

In the SMU upset, UT's defense limited Kyle Rote to three yards on seven carries. And Ben Procter had perhaps his greatest moment when he caught the winning pass, a 26-yarder in the upset. Cherry was carried off the field by his players following the upset.

One-Eyed Dillon

In 1950, a week after the SMU upset, UT safety Bobby Dillon from Temple sparked a 27-20 victory over Baylor. And he did it with one eye. Dillon lost his left eye in 1940 at the age of 10.

"I started having trouble with my eye when I was about five years old," Dillon said. "And I had to have it taken out in 1940 when I shattered the left lens of my spectacles while helping the neighbors move." Doctors fitted him with an artificial eye.

In 1950, Dillon averaged 22.3 yards per punt return. With the score tied 20-20, Dillon fielded a punt and returned it 85 yards for a touchdown and the winning score. He also intercepted a pass on SMU's last drive.

Changing of the Guard

Cherry coached only four seasons and resigned because he suffered from insomnia and ulcers in 1950. He entered the oil business with his brother Alton W. Cherry of Dallas, because it improved the family's financial standing. He later wrote an article in *The Saturday Evening Post*, "Why I Quit Football."

Word leaked out that Cherry was going to quit, so he announced his departure. But the team still went on to win the SWC title before losing to Tennessee in the Cotton Bowl.

"It was soul-satisfying to wind up as the coach of a champion in December after hearing the wolves well into October," Cherry wrote in *The Post.*

He also wrote: "I am no longer interested in trying to please the public with a professional show put on by a bunch of semipros operating under rules."

Intimidating McFadin

In 1951, the Korean War had started. Bud McFadin, UT's All-America tackle, was playing for the Carswell Air Force Base team, which was composed of great players from all over the country. The Carswell team traveled to Southern Mississippi to play.

"Our coach 'Pie' Vann called in Pat Ferlise [a lineman]," remembers Jimmie McDowell, the Southern Mississippi athletic publicity director at the time. "And he said, 'Pat, you have to play against McFadin Saturday night.' Pat weighed 185 pounds. Coach Pie said, 'The last thing you want to do is make that big son of a gun mad.'

"As the game approached, Pat began to wonder, 'How tough is Bud McFadin?'" McDowell recalled. "He thought he would just find out on the first play. They didn't wear facemasks in those days. Pat jumped the gun and gave McFadin his best forearm in the face. And Bud didn't even blink. And that left about 59 minutes to go. Pat looked up at Bud and said, 'Excuse me.'"

Carswell won 40-0.

Tough-Man Title to Sewell

Harley Sewell, an All-America middle guard who played for UT from 1950 to 1952, was called "the toughest man who ever played for the Longhorns" by longtime UT trainer Frank Medina.

Medina told the *Houston Post:* "People talk about Bud McFadin, Scott Appleton and Tommy Nobis, but Sewell was the toughest boy since I have been here. He was the most indestructible player as well as the most consistent. There were never any hot or cold days for Harley. He established a norm and kept it."

As an example, Sewell and teammate Don Menasco tackled an Oklahoma player in the end zone for a safety in their annual game in Dallas. In the process, they smashed the two-by-four Cotton Bowl goalposts.

The Recruitment of Sewell

Former UT player Phil Bolin, a guard on the Longhorns' 1943 SWC championship team, was driving down a country road in North Texas around 1950 when he saw Harley Sewell atop a telephone pole. Bolin always was looking for prospects for the

Guard Harley Sewell was recruited from the top of a telephone pole. *Cotton Bowl Athletic Association*

Longhorns and had been told about Sewell, who was working on the telephone line.

The story goes this way:

"Son," Bolin yelled at Sewell atop the pole, "how would you like to play football for the University of Texas?"

"Be fine," Sewell responded.

Sewell told Bolin he had played football at Saint Jo High School (fullback and tackle on defense). Sewell visited Austin and was convinced to spend the night. Austin's biggest lure was the Hill Hall food. Later UT coach Blair Cherry sent Sewell a postcard offering him a scholarship.

But UT assistant coach J.T. King had to convince him to stay after getting a call from Sewell's roommate. Sewell said he was homesick. King said Sewell was packing his old cardboard suitcase, but he was talking and pitching clothes out of it as fast as Sewell could put them in it. Finally King won out.

Hook 'Em Begins

The tradition of "Hook 'Em Horns" was developed in 1955, the evening before Jim Swink led eighth-ranked TCU to a 47-20 romp over the Longhorns in Austin.

Harley Clark, UT's head cheerleader, was at a pep rally at Gregory Gym and discovered the school didn't have a formal sign.

So he showed the rally how to create the Longhorn head by tucking the middle and ring finger under the thumb and at the same time leaving the little and index finger extended.

Bang the Drum Loudly

Big Bertha was presented to the Longhorn Band in 1955 by Colonel D. Harold Byrd, a prominent Dallas oilman and honorary Longhorn Band president. Byrd got the drum for one dollar from the University of Chicago after it had been retired from the football scene years earlier. It was actually being displayed as a museum piece in Indiana.

The University of Chicago Maroons had phased out football in the late 1930s and no longer had a need for it. Big Bertha is eight feet in diameter and 44 inches wide, and weighs 500 pounds. It was made in 1922 by a music company in Elkhart, Indiana. The owner was a University of Chicago alum who was looking for a bigger drum than Purdue's. He donated the huge drum to the University of Chicago.

CHAPTER FOUR

Darrell
Royal Magic

Arkansas Series Heats up

Texas's fortunes started to change dramatically when a young Oklahoman named Darrell Royal became the Longhorns' coach in 1957 and built a dynasty in Austin. Before he coached at Texas, OU graduate Royal became a head coach in the Canadian Football League at the age of 28 and later served head coaching stints at Mississippi State and Washington en route to Texas. Royal retired from coaching in 1976, taking over as UT's athletic director.

"I can tell you as early as my junior high days, I knew I wanted to coach the game," Royal said.

Leaving Mississippi

In 1955, the University of Houston was trying to get a big-time football schedule. So they sent four planes across the South to pick up athletic directors, head football coaches, and sports editors to promote the school.

One of the planes came to Jackson, Mississippi. Darrell Royal, the head coach at Mississippi State, was on the plane with Ole Miss coach Johnny Vaught and Tadpole Smith, the athletic director at Ole Miss. Jimmie McDowell, then the sports editor at the *Jackson Daily News,* was on the flight as well.

They all headed to Aransas Pass off the Gulf Coast of Texas.

"We went on this flight to right outside of Corpus Christi where they have great deep-sea fishing," McDowell recalled. "They had a game of chance the night before the guys went out fishing. And then the next day Vaught somehow catches a fish by the tail and somehow lands him, despite the night before there being a big storm."

Royal called Vaught the "Big Possum."

According to McDowell, Royal said, "That 'Big Possum' whips you in football, wins your money in a game of chance, and catches a fish by the tail. I am getting the hell out of Mississippi."

Royal the Sportscaster

True to his word, Royal left Mississippi after the 1955 season to take the Washington job. He lasted in Seattle one year before taking the Texas job.

Royal stopped off in Dallas for the Cotton Bowl game on January 1, 1957, between TCU and Syracuse. Little did he know that three years later he would be leading Texas into the Cotton Bowl against that same Syracuse team.

"TCU and Syracuse were playing, and Jim Brown had that great day," Royal said years later. "I worked in the booth with Tom Harmon during the national radio broadcast and did the so-called color. So I saw the great day Jim [Brown] had that afternoon."

TCU won the game 28-27, but Jim Brown ran for 132 yards, scored three touchdowns, and kicked three extra points.

Medina: Neat and Tidy

In 1945 Frank Medina was brought to Texas as trainer by D.X. Bible. He would later serve twice as head trainer for the U.S. Olympic team. The four-foot-10 Cherokee Indian was head trainer at UT from 1945 to 1977 before suffering a stroke.

He carried out Royal's locker room orders and players' personal grooming standards to a "T."

"Neatness and organization are the trademark of Darrell's teams," Medina said in a 1968 interview in the *Houston Post.* "We want them well groomed on and off the field. We dress them in the best football equipment and stress the importance of appearance.

"There is no smutty or foul talk here in the training room or elsewhere. We don't tolerate it. In our dining room we serve the finest food. We demand that the dorm rooms stay clean. And no longer are players ashamed to show parents where they live."

Royal's Rookie Season

In Royal's first season, 1957, Texas played six nationally ranked teams, including Ole Miss (39-7 loss) in the Sugar Bowl, and went 4-2 in those games. Royal's first UT team upset Bear Bryant's last Texas A&M team 9-7, when Bobby Lackey kicked the winning field goal.

Walter Fondren III was the best player on Royal's first team in 1957. He could throw the running pass in the Split-T option. As a sophomore he was compared to SMU's Doak Walker because of his punting, returning, passing and running skills. But UT was only 5-5 and 1-9 his first two seasons of 1955 and 1956.

Fondren played in the single wing and was a more featured player. He was a millionaire-to-be with his family owning interest in Humble Oil. Fondren's grandfather helped found the company. His family had donated library buildings to schools. Jokes were that Royal was looking into NCAA rules to see if it was OK for the coach to ride in his player's personal airplane.

Royal was trying to develop Fondren into what he calls a "city runner: north and south"—instead of a—"rural runner: east and west."

Moving up

Royal's first team in the 1957 season (6-4-1) reversed Texas football fortunes from a 1-9 season in 1956. And in 1959 Texas tied for Royal's first Southwest Conference title.

Quarterback Bobby Lackey led UT on a winning 90-yard drive to beat Texas A&M 20-17 in College Station and gain a berth in the Cotton Bowl. Lackey was the lanky six-foot-three, 205-pound star on Royal's first three teams at UT.

Central Figure: Mike Cotton

UT quarterback Mike Cotton was a neighbor of Darrell Royal's while in high school and never considered attending another school.

In 1958 Cotton led the UT freshmen to an unbeaten season, their first since 1941. He shared quarterbacking duties with Bobby Lackey as a sophomore in 1959 and took over quarterback as a junior in 1960.

He was elected co-captain as a senior in 1961 and directed the famous Flip-Flop offense. James Saxton was the All-America tailback who sat out most of the second halves while the UT reserves racked up points.

"Recruiting was tough that year," Royal said of the player who lived four houses down from him. "I had to hurry home from the office or a trip to check up on Mike [who was All-American as a senior from Austin] to see who had been visiting him. But the neighbors were real nice. They kept me posted. I don't believe Mike visited another campus."

Texas-Arkansas Rivalry

In 1894, Texas won the first meeting 54-0. Arkansas lost the first 14 games of the series. Not until 1933 did Arkansas register a victory (20-6). But the rivalry didn't hit its zenith until the Darrell Royal-Frank Broyles coaching matchups starting in 1958. Broyles became Arkansas's coach that season, and they both retired from coaching after playing each other in 1976.

During those 19 years, 10 games decided which of the two teams would represent the Southwest Conference in the Cotton Bowl. On 11 occasions, both teams were ranked in the top 20 entering the game. And six times both were in the top 10.

Crying for the Hogs

In 1960, Broyles picked up his first victory over Texas 24-23 in Austin and remembers he knew how important the game was to the state of Arkansas.

His team and fans cried when the Razorbacks returned home to Fayetteville, Arkansas.

"We had to deplane at the end of the runway," Broyles remembers, because of the mob at the airport to greet the victorious Hogs. "I got a good indication of just how important it was to beat Texas."

Arkansas beat Texas on Mickey Cissell's field goal with 25 seconds remaining.

The defeat was draining for Texas, which lost the next week to Rice 7-0. The Longhorns fell out of the ratings and wound up in the Bluebonnet Bowl, where they tied Alabama 3-3.

Getting to No. 1

A 27-0 victory over SMU on November 24, 1961, propelled Texas (7-0) to a No. 1 ranking for the first time in school history. Texas went into the game ranked No. 3, but higher-ranked Michigan State and Ole Miss both lost that day.

James Saxton rushed for 173 yards on 16 carries to key the victory, picking up 80 of those yards on a touchdown run that put Texas on the board in the third quarter after a scoreless first half.

"An average back would have been stopped at the line of scrimmage," SMU coach Bill Meek said of the run after the game. "A good back might have made five yards."

Then Falling

But two weeks later, a 6-0 loss to TCU in Austin knocked Texas out of a chance to play for the national championship. Saxton got hurt early in the game and wasn't a factor, seriously crippling Texas's attack.

Coach Darrell Royal and quarterback Duke Carlisle were
a tough combination to beat in the 1964 Cotton Bowl
game against Navy. UT won 28-6. *Cotton Bowl Athletic Association*

"It was disappointing, a terrible loss," said UT quarterback
Duke Carlisle. "It was probably the most disappointing game while
I was at Texas."

Twelve days later Texas regrouped to beat Texas A&M 25-0,
earning a tie for the Southwest Conference title and a berth in the
Cotton Bowl, where the Longhorns knocked off Ole Miss 12-7.

Wear Those Pads

Texas beat Oregon 25-13 in the 1962 season opener. Mel
Renfro was returning punts for Oregon. UT tackle Scott Appleton,

who won the Outland Trophy in 1963, was exposed as not wearing a piece of equipment on the play.

"Scott Appleton and I both were running toward him," remembers David McWilliams, a member of the 1962 team and later a UT head coach. "Renfro put a juke on us and ran around us. Appleton turned and somebody hit him. And he got a hip pointer. And the reason I remember it, Scott wasn't wearing hip pads because he thought it would make him faster. And did Coach Royal go after him. He wore them from then on."

Appleton wasn't usually caught off guard.

"They moved him to what we call now defensive guard as a freshman," McWilliams said. "We played that wide tackle six. They call them tackles now. And he made as many plays on the freshman team as the linebackers did. He was probably as flexible as anybody I have ever seen. He was a tremendous player against the run. In the pros, his biggest problem was rushing the passer."

The Jarring Fumble

Perhaps the most famous Texas hit, tackle, and fumble occurred against Arkansas during the 1962 season. Texas had ascended to a No. 1 ranking after a 9-6 victory over Oklahoma.

Arkansas was leading No. 1 Texas 3-0 and was preparing to go in for another score in the third quarter. UT linebacker Johnny Treadwell was yelling at his teammates.

Linebacker Pat Culpepper recounted this incident to the *Houston Chronicle* in 1993.

"Dammit, get your head up," Treadwell said. "We've got them right where we want them. They have run out of room. They can't throw a long pass. They've got to come right at us."

Two plays later, Culpepper and Treadwell were part of a hit on Arkansas fullback Danny Brabham, who fumbled into the end zone. The Longhorns recovered for a touchback. Late in the game, Texas put together a 90-yard drive and went on to win 7-3 and preserve its top ranking.

"If Brabham doesn't fumble, he goes over, or so close to it, we go over on the next play," Arkansas coach Frank Broyles said. "And that's the ballgame. [Brabham] didn't fumble. He was just knocked loose from the ball. Culpepper did it. He tore Brabham's head off. He was running a little too high."

No Surprise

Linebacker Pat Culpepper was a little bowling ball at five foot nine and 193 pounds. The hit on Brabham was just an example of his ferocious play.

"He played every inch to his capabilities," Royal said. "An athlete cannot help it if he isn't six foot four and weighs 250 pounds or can run under 10 seconds. The only things of which he has 100 percent control are aggressiveness, desire, and effort. Pat has mastered these things. And that's the most complimentary thing you can say about a boy.

"If every college football player in America played like Pat, football probably would be banned. He plays that hard. And yet he is the finest youngster ever to play the game. He never took unfair advantage of an opponent."

A Better Idea with Ford

Texas put together a 90-yard drive to finally score with 36 seconds remaining to beat Arkansas 7-3.

Scatback Tommy Ford—five foot nine, 183 pounds—scored from the three-yard line, capping the 20-play drive. His running usually came off the 18 Sweep during the Flip-Flop offense of the early 1960s.

On third and four, Ford caught a flat pass and drove hard to make a first down by inches. On the touchdown run, he was met by two defenders, but he drove them back into the end zone.

"I know I was in the huddle," UT's center David McWilliams said. "I don't remember who came in with the play. It was an offensive lineman. The call was '18 Sweep.' He said, 'Coach Royal said if we don't make it we will go for a field goal.' There was a lot of cursing going on in the huddle that we weren't kicking a field goal. We knew if we didn't make it, we were going to call a timeout and talk about it. I often wondered if he added that on there, but I have never asked him.

"Here's the biggest play of the game for us, and he gives the ball to Ford on the power sweep," McWilliams added. "That tells you a little bit about the runner he is. I remember Ford got hit about the two-yard line and ran over a couple of guys."

The next week in a 14-14 tie with Rice, Ford scored from three yards out and carried six times during a 62-yard drive to tie the score at 7-7. In the third quarter, Ford returned a Rice punt 55 yards to the Owls' nine to set up UT's second score.

"When Tommy heads up the stovepipe, he heads for home," said UT offensive backfield coach Bill Ellington.

"I couldn't talk about a game," UT coach Darrell Royal said. "I'd have to talk about his games. He's never had a bad game.... He'd stick his head in a buzz saw."

Keys to Coach Royal

"Detail. It had to be done exactly right," David McWilliams said. "I am talking offense and defense. Plus, he expected you to handle yourself on the field and not get those unnecessary penalties.

"I remember one time it was early in the game and they sent in the backup center. I wondered what did I do wrong? Coach Royal, as I was coming off the field, waved me down there. I went down and I was kind of scared. You don't normally substitute one guy.

"I said, 'Yes sir.'

"He said, 'Your jersey is sticking out. Go back there and put it in.'

"So I went back there and got a group of guys around and undid my pants and stuck my jersey in there. And I went back to him. And he said, 'All right. Get back in.' That was detail. That was pride.

"The other thing he taught me was football was a game of contact," McWilliams said. "In our practice we had a lot of contact, cull drills and a lot of hitting. You learned if you wanted to get on that football field, you had to be a hitter. Good clean hits, but nothing dirty."

That Senior Class

The 1963 seniors felt that they had let national championships slip through their hands during their sophomore and junior seasons with a 6-0 loss to TCU in 1961 and a 14-14 tie with Rice in 1962. The 13-0 loss to LSU in the 1963 Cotton Bowl was also fresh in the players' minds.

"I think going into the '63 season, there was a lot of conversation, we can't throw it away this year," David McWilliams said. "I remember times in 1963 when we were down, we would say remember, now, we are not going to lose this thing again."

The 1963 seniors would put together a perfect senior year (11-0) and win the national championship. And over a three-year period they would register 30 victories, two defeats, and a tie.

Appleton's Big Game

One of those seniors was tackle Scott Appleton, who was simply brilliant when he lined up against Oklahoma's Ralph Neely in 1963. In UT's 28-7 victory over the Sooners, Appleton made 18 tackles, caused one fumble that led to a score, and put pressure on the backs.

"I've got great memories about him," said David McWilliams, who was Appleton's roommate at Texas. "For three years there were probably not too many things we didn't do together. Every time you were around him he wanted to compete. It didn't matter if it was pitching quarters or flat-foot jumping; he was just a competitor.

"He would want to play limbo with the broom. He taught me more about competition. Yet if you beat him, he wasn't distraught. He loved to compete. I mean in everything. He would just make up games. If you went swimming, he would want to race you."

Baylor guard Mike Bourland said there was nothing dirty about his play.

"A tremendous player, one of the cleanest I have played against," Bourland said. "He never takes a false step. He may move around a block, but he never loses the ball and he never loses leverage on the blocker. If he feels he is losing leverage, he just fans out in the proper pursuit circle. I tried to stay high on my blocks. If I went for his legs, he'd just have gone around me."

Biggest Defensive Play of 1963

Quarterback Duke Carlisle actually made the biggest defensive play of the 1963 season when he substituted in at safety to save a 7-0 victory over Baylor.

Carlisle stole a pass from Baylor's Lawrence Elkins in the end zone with 19 seconds remaining. Baylor quarterback Don Trull threw the pass. But Carlisle snatched the ball from Elkins eight yards into the end zone. Elkins had run a post pattern and had eluded UT defender Joe Dixon.

Carlisle had closed nearly 15 yards after the ball left Trull's hand. Texas then knelt with the ball on the next play, and the game was over.

"Thank you, Duke, you saved my life," Dixon told Carlisle after the game.

"The prior year I played a lot of defense, but that year I played only offense," Carlisle said. "We fumbled deep in our own territory. What normally happened, I would leave the game and another player would come in and play safety. At the time, I looked at the sideline, and no one came in. So I played the rest of the game."

Carlisle said UT defensive coordinator Mike Campbell made a spur-of-the-moment decision that he was to stay in the game for Jim Hudson, who went on to play for the New York Jets.

"[As the play developed] I looked back at Trull, and he was looking over my shoulder, so I took off that way," Carlisle said. "We were on our own 20, so they were limited how deep a pattern they could run. I had time to get back in the end zone. It was pretty remarkable we held that Baylor team scoreless."

Another Close Call

The final game of the 1963 season was a 15-13 victory over Texas A&M in College Station. That capped off a 10-0 regular season and sent the top-ranked Longhorns into the 1964 Cotton Bowl game against Navy and Roger Staubach.

"I remember the field was soaking wet," McWilliams said. "To my knowledge it hadn't rained all week. I believe we were down 13-3 and Coach Royal put quarterback Tommy Wade in and he drove us down to the goal line and they took him out and put Duke Carlisle in and he scored.

"On another drive we threw an interception, the A&M guy tried to lateral to one of the other A&M guys, and we slapped it down and recovered it and it gave us another first down. From there, Wade drove us down and then we put Carlisle back in and we ran a quarterback sneak. I was playing center. We won the game."

Short-Yardage Back

In 1963, Tommy Ford, the "Texas T Bird," averaged 4.6 yards per carry his senior season and scored nine touchdowns. He was called "the best five-yard runner in SWC history" by one league coach.

Ford, from San Angelo, would practice spin moves, timing it just right so that he could spin at just the right moment. Ford told Blackie Sherrod of Dallas that he learned something from LSU's Jerry Stovall in the previous year's loss to the Tigers in the Cotton Bowl.

"He has a knack of putting his hand on the ground when he is knocked off balance and going down," Ford told Sherrod. "He'll stick his hand out and run a few steps with it on the ground and push himself back in balance. I've practiced that."

"Someone my senior year asked me who was the toughest back I have ever tackled," McWilliams said. "I'd say Tommy Ford in spring practice because he would kick you, he would elbow you. He would do whatever he had to do to make his yards. They say he averaged five yards a carry. And we would say that's all we would block him. Actually, we would block them three yards, and he would knock them two yards."

Ford usually went through two or three helmets a season because of his battering-ram style of running.

Tommy Nobis helped stop Joe Namath short of the goal line in a key play during UT's 1965 Orange Bowl victory over Alabama. *Cotton Bowl Athletic Association*

The Nobis Legend

Tommy Nobis, who would later win the Outland Trophy as a senior in 1965, was the only sophomore in the starting lineup of the 1963 national champions and played both offensive guard and linebacker. He played offense and defense throughout his career.

"When Nobis came along," David McWilliams said, "we had a senior ball club. We only had two sophomores playing, and one of them was Tommy Nobis and the other was Phil Harris. Nobis reminded me a lot of Scott Appleton, because he was a great competitor. He only weighed about 190 pounds. He was kinda bow-legged and real quiet. He was just the quietest guy. I thought John Treadwell could hit you with a forearm. But Nobis just had the instinct for finding the ball."

"If we were going to have a winning team, we're going to spend most of our time on offense," Royal told the *San Antonio Express-News*. "If Nobis played just defense, he's going to be out there just half the time. You gotta be crazy having Nobis play less than half the game."

Nobis was drafted by the Atlanta Falcons in the first round of the 1966 NFL draft and was All-Pro five of 11 seasons.

One-Blemish Season

UT's only loss of the 1964 season was 14-13 to Arkansas in Austin. Ernie Koy carried the ball 27 times for 110 yards and scored a touchdown. That loss to No. 8 Arkansas snapped a 15-game winning streak and knocked the Longhorns from the No. 1 ranking in the country.

Arkansas would go on to win a national championship (Football Writers Association of America) after beating Nebraska 10-7 in the Cotton Bowl.

No. 8 Arkansas went ahead midway through the fourth quarter, but Texas took the ball and went 70 yards to score with 1:27 left. Trailing 14-13, UT elected to go for two points and the victory, but Marvin Kristynik's pass fell incomplete at the goal line.

Arkansas's Ken Hatfield, who would later coach the Razorbacks, returned a punt 81 yards for a touchdown. That was the difference in the game. It was one of the two most painful losses for Royal during the series.

"We had covered the kick, and a guy substituting was not off the field," Royal remembers. "Then on the next one, [Hatfield] returned it all the way."

Consolation Prize

Texas still got to go to a major bowl game as second-place finisher in the 1964 Southwest Conference race. And it turned out to be a classic game at the Orange Bowl against Alabama.

One of the most dramatic and controversial goal-line stands in UT history occurred in the final quarter of UT's 21-17 victory over No. 1-ranked Alabama in the 1965 Orange Bowl.

Alabama, behind gimpy-kneed quarterback Joe Namath, had effectively passed its way down to the UT six, trailing only by the final score. Years later UT linebacker Tommy Nobis said he was baffled that Namath didn't keep passing. Instead, Alabama ran the ball at the middle of the Longhorns' defense when it got close to the goal line.

Three running plays later, Alabama was at the one on fourth down. Shockingly, Namath, who was even doubtful before the game with a knee injury, carried the ball on a quarterback sneak. Nobis and other UT players Diron Talbert, Frank Bedrick, and Tommie Currie stopped Namath just short, although with a second effort he did get over. Officials ruled he was already down. Neither team scored again, although Namath had two more possessions in the game.

"A lot of my friends have said to me over the years, 'Joe, you scored on that play,'" Namath recounted in *Fifty Years at the Fifty: The Orange Bowl Story.* "I always say the same thing and have for years, 'No, I didn't score, but I was over the goal line.'"

The Koy Connection

Ernie A. Koy was a three-time All-Southwest Conference running back at Texas from 1930 to 1932. His son was Ernie M. Koy, who played for the Longhorns from 1962 to 1964, was a wingback (1962), fullback (1963), and tailback (1964). He also was a great punter, with a 39.2 average in 1962 and a 38.4 average in 1964.

He spurred the Longhorns upset of Alabama in the 1965 Orange Bowl with 133 yards rushing.

The elder Koy played baseball and later was in the major leagues. He came to Texas unheralded after not playing football in high school and went out for the Texas team on his own. The younger Ernie was recruited by more than 50 schools.

"Ernie [M.] Koy is the greatest punter in the nation, college or pro," wrote former Army coach Red Blaik in a guest column for a Houston newspaper. "He averages 48 yards per kick and hangs the ball in the air for five seconds every time he boots one. Texas does not attempt to punt out of bounds. The Longhorns want the defense to handle the ball, figuring sooner or later some unfortunate safety man will fumble in the middle of a knot of Texas tacklers."

Another son, Ted Koy, played from 1967 to 1969. And Robert Koy, son of Ernie M., lettered for UT in 1999.

Another Tough Arkansas Loss

In 1965, Texas suffered a second straight close loss to Arkansas 27-24 in Fayetteville. Texas entered the game ranked No. 1 for a second straight year. That loss started a three-game UT tailspin, which included losses to Rice and SMU and saw UT fall out of the ratings and finish in a tie for fourth in the SWC.

Again, UT quarterback Marvin Kristynik was a central figure when he rallied his team from 20-0 down. A field goal with four minutes remaining gave UT a 24-20 lead, but Arkansas quarterback Jon Brittenum led the Hogs to the winning score with 1:32 remaining in the game.

"[The game in] 1965 was even tougher [than the 1964 loss]," UT coach Darrell Royal said. "They went up 20-0. We fought back to go ahead 24-20, but then they went 80 yards and moved right down the field [to win 27-24]."

Salvaging the Season

Texas entered the season-ending 1965 Texas A&M game in College Station with a 5-4 record. And the Longhorns trailed 17-0 at halftime.

The Aggies utilized a dazzling play designed by coach Gene Stallings called the "Texas Special" as part of a dominating first half by the team.

Stallings had Aggies quarterback Harry Ledbetter toss a lateral to wide receiver Jim Kauffman. He then threw a pass to Ken McLean, who caught the ball and went 91 yards for a touchdown.

"It was one of the most original, most clever plays I've ever seen," Royal said at the time.

"Coach Royal told us at halftime he could put all kind of diagrams on the board, but they wouldn't help," UT quarterback Marvin Kristynik said. "It was just a matter of whether we wanted to win or not. Then he wrote 21-17 on the blackboard and said, 'That's what we can do.' And we did."

CHAPTER FIVE

Glory Days Continue with the Wishbone

As the 1960s wore on, Texas endured three straight four-loss seasons from 1965 to 1967, but that all changed in 1968 when Texas installed the Wishbone offense. It produced two more national championships and a 30-game winning streak that rocked the college football world.

Texas's Best Athlete?

Entering the era of the Wishbone, UT still had a strong defensive team. Witness the presence of defensive back Bill Bradley, who played from 1966 to 1968 and was the team captain his senior year.

In his last regular-season game against Texas A&M in 1968, Bradley intercepted four passes, the most in UT history. From 1966 to 1968, Bradley led Texas in punting.

Bradley was selected in the third round of the 1969 NFL draft by the Philadelphia Eagles and had a successful career there.

"The best athlete was Bill Bradley," Texas coach Fred Akers said. "Bill could do more things better than anyone I ever saw. I think he was the best all-around athlete. Bradley was recruited by every school in the Southwest Conference for football, basketball, baseball, and track. He was also a great punter."

"Super Bill" Bradley, who played four positions for Texas (quarterback, defensive back, punter, and wide receiver), was the original Wishbone quarterback for the Longhorns in the season opener in 1968. But he was eventually replaced by James Street.

Coffee Shop Talk

Quarterback Eddie Phillips, who would start and run the Wishbone after James Street's career was over, remembers the fall of 1968 and the new offense being introduced.

"I remember coach [Emory] Bellard taking us someplace and we had breakfast," Phillips said. "He got the pepper and salt shakers and had this god-awful lineup. The first scheme had the fullback a little too close to the quarterback to hit the hole real quickly. But the fullback had to have a little bit of vision, so they backed him up a little bit. The first year we ran it, offenses had so much trouble picking it up."

Fred Akers, a Texas assistant coach in those days, said the Wishbone allowed more good athletes on the field for Texas.

"Those running backs were really good football players, and they needed to be out there," Akers said. "That was about the only way you could keep them there and still have somewhat of an open offense. It was the first time in football you could have a running back wide toward the split end. You didn't count on him being a blocker as much as the linemen and the backs."

The Premature Unveiling

Fourth-ranked Texas unveiled the Wishbone offense in a 20-20 tie with No. 11-ranked Houston in the 1968 season opener in Austin. Texas had closed practices, and mum was the word, or so Texas coaches believed about their plans.

But Ted Nance, a former Houston sports information director, relayed the story of how the Wishbone became known to Houston coaches before the game.

"The sister of one of our players had a boyfriend who played for Texas, and she mentioned to her brother that Texas had a new offense that looked like a Y offense," Nance recalled. "[Houston coach] Bill Yeoman had invented the Veer offense in 1964. And the Wishbone was really just a variation of the Veer. Instead of a flanker, the Wishbone brought the flanker into the backfield. But the Wishbone option was similar to ours, so the offense did not present as much of a problem to us as it did the rest of the Texas opponents later that year."

The night before the game, Texas played host to a press party. And Harry Kalas, one of Houston's play-by-play announcers, had received a diagram of UT's Wishbone offense from the Houston coaches to help him prepare for the game.

"At the press party, Kalas, unaware that Texas had been having closed practices, went up to Royal, showed him the play, and asked him what he called it," Nance said. "Needless to say, Royal was upset and wanted to know how he knew about it. The next night, after the game, Mickey Herskowitz [of the *Houston Post*] called the offense the Wishbone, and it stuck. Ironically, a UH graduate had named the Texas offense."

The Original Backfield, Then Street

Coach Darrell Royal's original Wishbone backfield had Bill Bradley at quarterback, Steve Worster at fullback, and Chris Gilbert and Ted Koy at the halfback spots.

After a 31-22 loss to Texas Tech, a 31-3 win over Oklahoma State began the 30-game winning streak. And quarterback James Street made his first start against Oklahoma State. He had come off the bench and played well the week before in the loss in Lubbock. He would post a 20-0 record as a starter during the 1968 and 1969 seasons.

"In the Wishbone, all you had to do was be a little afraid," Street said. "Every time they are going to hit, you just pitch the ball.

I want to personally thank Coach Royal for giving a skinny kid from Longview the opportunity to come to the University of Texas and play football. I was very fortunate to be at the right place at the right time. They put the offense in to fit my style, and the rest is history."

Against Oklahoma State, Street engineered a eight-play 70-yard drive in the third quarter to push UT ahead 17-3. Street connected on a four-yard pass with Bill Bradley to give Texas a 24-3 lead. Street finished with 140 yards passing and two touchdowns.

The next week, Texas beat Oklahoma in Dallas 26-20.

"Oklahoma was really the turning point for the team," Gilbert said that season. "That gave us confidence in James [Street]."

Street-Royal Relationship

Quarterback James Street remembers Royal getting the yellow legal pad and diagramming the Wishbone. But it was just one of the innovations he remembers from Royal, who was a very unique individual.

"He was the first in the nation to have an academic counselor," Street said. "A 'T' ring is given to every letterman who earns a degree.

"He came from a background where all you had was your integrity and character," Street added. "He was not a rah-rah coach. He would not give a big-game speech. He said attention to detail, kicking game, and the breaks would win the game. He didn't get real close to his players. But I learned so much.

"He told me to just take care of every play. Play every play like it is a big play and winning will take care of itself."

Gilbert into the Record Book

UT's Chris Gilbert became the first player in NCAA history to rush for 1,000 yards in three straight seasons from 1966 to 1968. In those days freshmen were not eligible for the varsity, or he might have done it in four straight seasons.

Gilbert only rushed in the famed Wishbone his senior season, but overall the five-foot-10, 180-pound running back rushed for 100 or more yards in half of his 30 regular-season games.

In his senior season in the Wishbone, he rushed for 1,132 yards and 13 touchdowns and averaged 6.2 yards per carry from the left halfback spot. He also caught 11 passes for 204 yards and two touchdowns and returned kickoffs.

In 1967, as a junior, he rushed 96 yards for a touchdown against TCU. Through the 2004 season that still ranks as the longest rushing play in Texas history.

Records Fall

Texas's Wishbone broke six Southwest Conference team records in 1968 alone. It was just getting started in a groove.

"It was an offense of precision, timing, beauty, of smash-mouth, ball-control, running-oriented offense, which makes sense for a Darrell Royal-coached team," said split end Cotton Speyrer. "Coach Royal had a philosophy about the passing game. When you throw the ball, three things could happen, and two of them are bad. I was a split end in that great running/non-passing offense. In most games, I was more likely to catch a cold than to catch a pass."

During the 1969 and 1970 seasons, the results were even better than in 1968 when UT averaged 313.5 yards per game rushing. Texas led the nation in rushing with 363 yards a game in 1969 and 374.5 yards a contest in 1970.

"Any offense probably would have been successful with the people we had," said Eddie Phillips, who took over as UT's quarterback in the 1970 season. "The Wishbone fit the personalities and strengths of our team. We had gifted athletes at running back, a quarterback who could throw a little bit, and a good offensive line."

The Shootout: No. 1 Texas vs. No. 2 Arkansas

The 1969 game in Fayetteville, Arkansas, had all the trappings of a political rally. President Richard Nixon was in attendance, and future President George H.W. Bush was there as well.

The game had been arranged by Beano Cook of ABC. He had moved the game from the normal October date to the first week of December. It was a brilliant Madison Avenue move on the part of

Cook, because both teams entered the game unbeaten and untied for the Shootout in the 100th year of college football.

It took Michigan's upset of Ohio State the previous week to set up the national championship showdown between the old Southwest Conference rivals.

Arkansas's Frank Broyles has never looked at a film of the 1969 game. He doesn't have to, because the play of the century is still embedded in his mind.

The Play

Broyles calls UT's fourth-down pass to tight end Randy Peschel, "a brilliant call" by Royal and his staff. Arkansas's Chuck Dicus said, "What a strange call for a Wishbone team in a critical situation." Texas trailed 14-8 at the time.

Fourth and three at the UT 43, quarterback James Street found Peschel on a 44-yard pass play to the Arkansas 13. That set up an 11-yard run by Ted Koy and then the tying score by Jim Bertelsen from two yards out. The winning extra point was kicked by Happy Feller, but only after third-string quarterback Donnie Wigginton made a save on a high snap.

There was 3:58 left to play. And Arkansas could not get into field goal range to win the game.

"[Street] was the killer," Broyles said. "The team always responded about 25 percent above their potential when he was leading the team."

"We did not catch them off guard," former UT coach Darrell Royal said about the pass to Peschel. "There were two defenders there. There were six hands there; two of them were ours and four of them were theirs. I am not sure one of their players didn't graze the ball.... It was like dropping the ball in a bucket."

Shootout Strategy

With his team behind 14-8, Royal did not believe Texas could run the ball down the field and win. Texas needed a gamble and a big pass play, which it got.

Quarterback James Street was a clutch performer in big games, like this Cotton Bowl meeting with Notre Dame in 1970, which Texas won 21-17.
Cotton Bowl Athletic Association

"Little did we expect that he would go to the tight end side, which they seldom did," Broyles said in a 1999 interview with *The Dallas Morning News.* "They threw some, but most of their passes were to the other side. That was another reason it was a great call. It was away from what their pattern of throwing the ball had been in the other nine games."

Peschel had caught only 12 passes in the nine previous games before making an outstanding catch between Arkansas's Jerry Moore and Dennis Berner and took the ball to the Arkansas 13.

Terry Don Phillips, a player on the Arkansas team, said of the pass to Peschel: "We couldn't get much of a pass rush because we were already on the ground."

More Heroics

UT's Tom Campbell, son of UT's defensive coordinator, made an interception to seal the victory on Arkansas's final possession.

Arkansas, needing only a field goal to win, drove to the Texas 39 by picking up three first downs. On second and three, Bill Montgomery tried to find John Rees at the Texas 20, but Campbell intercepted right in front of the Texas bench with 1:13 remaining.

Tipping His Hat to Royal

"Greatest coach of the last 50 years—Darrell Royal," Frank Broyles said 25 years after he and Royal retired. "Darrell Royal was not only a great coach, he was a complete coach. If I was an athletic director, I would want him as the coach. If I was the president, I would want him as the coach. If I was the head of the board of trustees, I would want him to be the coach. And if I was a fan, I would like for him to be the coach, because I would like to win."

Little Recalls Prediction

Bill Little, longtime UT sports publicist, recalls rooming with San Antonio newspaper columnist Dan Cook in Fayetteville before the Shootout. Cook, president of the Texas Sports Writers Association at the time, couldn't get a commercial flight into Fayetteville, either, so he rode on the team plane.

At 3 a.m. the day of the game, Little and Cook were lying in their respective beds awake when Little made a prediction.

"I said, 'Dan, I figured out if we have to have one pass in the game who the hero would be.'

"He said, 'Who?'

"I said, 'Randy Peschel.'

"Cook thought I was a prognosticator. Of course, later that year in baseball, I predicted Peschel would get a hit and he struck out three times."

Going for Two

Trailing Arkansas 14-0 in the 1969 game, UT got a lift when Street ran 42 yards for a touchdown on the first play of the fourth quarter. He then scored on a two-point conversion to narrow Arkansas's lead to 14-8.

Royal said he wanted UT to have two chances to make the two points, so he decided the percentages were better trying for it the first time. If it got down to the final time and the score was 14-13, it would probably be more difficult.

He said he knew if it came down to a tie or going for two, he was going to go for two. "I felt like if you're No. 1, you ought to play to stay No. 1."

Royal met late into the night with his coaching staff and discussed what they would run on the two-point conversion play, asking defensive coordinator Mike Campbell what play gave UT's defense the most trouble (in the spring and in fall scrimmages). And Campbell told Royal it was the counter option. That's what Street ran.

Broyles Second-Guesses Himself

Frank Broyles, who was then the coach of the Razorbacks, questions a decision he made midway through the fourth quarter.

"The toughest decision to live with was that I threw the ball on third down rather than going for a field goal when a field goal would have been as good as a touchdown," Broyles said of when Texas trailed 14-8. "It was the first time our quarterback had thrown an interception in 109 passes. Rather than set up the field goal, we tried to score on third down. That's what everybody second-guessed us about."

Arkansas had driven to the UT seven. On third down, Arkansas quarterback Bill Montgomery threw slightly behind Chuck Dicus, who was streaking across the goal line. UT's Danny Lester raced in front of Dicus for the interception.

A No. 1 Controversy

Receiving pressure from undefeated Penn State, President Nixon said at halftime of the Shootout that maybe Penn State should get a shot at the winner of the 1969 Arkansas-Texas game. President Nixon wound up presenting Texas with a plaque as the No. 1 team in the nation.

In those days, the national champion was voted upon before the bowl games.

Texas was No. 1 in all the major polls, including the National Football Foundation's poll.

Texas beat Notre Dame in the Cotton Bowl following the season to at least preserve the president's honor. Texas's 1969 champions were the last all-white national championship team.

A No. 1 Button

In December 1969, Dallas's Longhorns fanatic Ken Capps received a button from his father, James, which read "Texas is No. 1" on Christmas Eve, less than a month after Texas had beaten Arkansas 15-14 . It was a gift from Santa Claus.

Capps still has the button, which is on display in his Orange Room, at his house in Highland Park.

"My dad died a year later of a heart attack at the age of 43," said Capps, who has shared the button with former UT coach Darrell Royal.

The Campbell Connection

During his 20 seasons at UT, Mike Campbell coached seven All-Americans and 43 All-Southwest Conference players at Texas. Campbell's three sons—twins, Mike and Tom, and Rusty—all played for the Longhorns. Tom and Mike played on the 1969 national championship team and Rusty on the 1970 and 1971 teams.

Tom was a linebacker, then an All-SWC defensive back and made game-saving interceptions in 1969 in Texas's big victories over Arkansas and Notre Dame. He also was the Cotton Bowl's MVP on defense in a 36-13 victory over Tennessee.

"When they get their headgears on, it's just about impossible to tell them [apart]," UT coach Darrell Royal said about the Campbell twins.

The Courage of Freddie Steinmark

Safety Freddie Steinmark started 20 of 22 games during the 1968 and 1969 seasons, including the Shootout victory over Arkansas. Six days later he was diagnosed with cancer in his left leg and had to have it amputated. Administrators at UT's basketball game versus UCLA at Pauley Pavilion actually cried.

The five-foot-10, 166-pound Steinmark, on crutches, was presented with the game ball by UT coach Darrell Royal several weeks later when the Longhorns defeated Notre Dame 21-17 in the Cotton Bowl. That winter, by the help of an artificial limb, Steinmark walked across the stage at the UT football banquet to accept his football letter jacket.

The 22-year-old Steinmark died on June 6, 1971, but not before he served what would have been his senior season as a student freshman coach for UT.

In 1972, before a game against Miami, Florida, the scoreboard at Memorial Stadium was dedicated in his memory.

Shootout II

On December 5, 1970, top-ranked Texas beat Arkansas, 42-7, in Shootout II. Leading 14-7, UT stopped Arkansas near the goal line and then went 99 yards for a 21-7 lead. UT won its 30th straight.

"Coach Broyles had a great statement when someone asked him what the score would have been had they scored on that goal-line stand," said UT quarterback Eddie Phillips, "He said, 'Oh, it would have been 42-14 instead of 42-7.'"

The "Worster Crowd"

Fullback Steve Worster rushed for 126 yards on 21 carries against Arkansas in his last regular-season game, which was UT's 30th straight victory. Worster was considered perhaps the top recruit in the nation in 1967 and was part of a UT recruiting class that compiled a 35-2-1 record during four seasons. It was known as the "Worster Crowd."

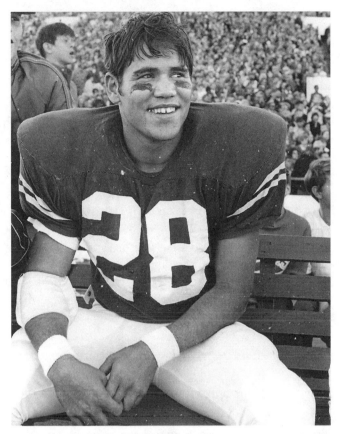

Freddie Steinmark has been an inspiration to Longhorns players for more than 30 years. *Cotton Bowl Athletic Association*

The Class of 1970 was 5-0 as part of the UT freshman team. Then came 9-1-1, 11-0, and 10-1 seasons. Quarterback Eddie Philips, a red-shirt junior in 1970, was a part of that class, which included Worster and others such as defensive end Bill Atessis and linebacker Scott Henderson.

Miraculous Finish

Texas nearly didn't make it to the 1970 Arkansas game unbeaten. It took a late pass play from quarterback Eddie Phillips to

Cotton Speyrer for No. 2 UT to beat No. 13 UCLA 20-17 in Austin.

Texas trailed 17-13 with 20 seconds remaining and faced a third-and-19 situation when Phillips found Speyrer for a 45-yard touchdown pass. Speyrer caught the ball at the 20 and raced into the end zone with 12 seconds remaining in the game.

"The interesting part of the game [was] the play before someone hit me and I fumbled it out of bounds and it stopped the clock," quarterback Eddie Phillips said. "That enabled me to throw the pass with a few seconds left."

Texas was hoping the safety would bite on a tight end crossing pattern, which only would be a decoy. The real target was Speyrer, running a deeper pattern.

"Our tight end, instead of going 15 yards, he went a little deeper," Phillips said. "It got the safety's attention, and he did bite a little bit. Cotton caught it, and the safety was not real far out of position, but as fast as Cotton was he had no trouble getting to the end zone."

Snapping the Wishbone

UCLA nearly beat Texas that day because it defended the Wishbone differently than any team had until that point. The offense was in its third season of existence, and teams were starting to devise strategies to at least slow it down.

"UCLA did something different on defense the Wishbone had never seen," said David McWilliams, UT's freshman coach that season. "Basically they took their end and ran him up on the pitch real quick and the cornerback or safety would come underneath the end when the quarterback kept it. After that game is when Coach Royal and Emory Bellard put in the loaded option. It added to the Wishbone because we had never played anybody who had played defense like that."

The UCLA defense basically allowed fullback Steve Worster his yardage. He gained 106 yards on 19 carries and kept the Longhorns close until the big pass play.

Fullback Steve Worster was an original member of UT's famed Wishbone backfield. *Cotton Bowl Athletic Association*

Bertelsen Migrates South

Jim Bertelsen (1969-1971) hailed from Hudson, Wisconsin, population 6,000. The five-foot-11, 200-pounder came to Texas as a weak blocker, but left it as perhaps the best blocking halfback since Harrison Stafford (1930-1932).

He blocked for fullback Steve Worster for two seasons.

"Most backs his caliber in high school are used to carrying the ball and justly so," said Emory Bellard, UT assistant coach at the time.

Bertelsen wound up at Texas because he didn't like the cold Wisconsin winters and he was fond of horses. Bertelsen had an aunt who lived in Grand Prairie, a suburb of Dallas. She bragged about her nephew to her boss, a dentist, and he notified UT coaches about Bertelsen.

"Bertelsen is a natural," said his high school coach Don Kadidlo, the head coach at Hudson.

Roosevelt Leaks was UT's first African-American superstar.
Cotton Bowl Athletic Association

"He could do extraordinary things. The first game he ever played as a sophomore, we started him at linebacker and he made 17 unassisted tackles. He's a heel runner and that's why he has such amazing balance."

During his three seasons at Texas, Bertelsen rushed for 33 touchdowns and 2,510 yards.

Another Royal Move that Paid off

Safety Alan Lowry was an All-Southwest Conference defensive back during the 1971 season. But as a senior in 1972, coach Darrell Royal made Lowry his starting quarterback in the Wishbone offense. Lowry also made all-SWC at quarterback as well.

Lowry led the Longhorns to another Southwest Conference title and scored the controversial winning touchdown in No. 7 Texas's 17-13 victory over Alabama in the Cotton Bowl. As a baseball player and punter, he was an all-around athlete. Lowry had been a quarterback in high school and ran the Veer offense, but when he got to Texas the Longhorns had plenty of quarterbacks, so he moved to defense.

Another aid for Lowry was the play of sophomore fullback Roosevelt Leaks, who rushed for 1,099 yards that season.

Breaking the Color Barrier

Roosevelt Leaks, a fullback-halfback, wasn't the first black player in the University of Texas football program. That honor belongs to Julius Whittier in the early 1970s.

Leaks, however, was the first black superstar at Texas. He played from 1972 to 1974 when he rushed for nearly 3,000 yards. He rushed for 1,099 yards as a sophomore and 1,415 as a junior before suffering a knee injury. That curtailed his running in 1974, Earl Campbell's freshman season.

In 1973, Lonnie Bennett, another black UT running back said of Leaks: "I think he has provided an image of a black superstar for us. It may not help us in recruiting today, but kids are growing up who now idolize him. In five years, it will make a big difference. That's what he has done for blacks here."

Topping the Record

Roosevelt Leaks ran for 342 yards against SMU in a 42-14 victory at the Cotton Bowl in 1973. He broke the Southwest Conference record of 287 yards rushing set by Texas A&M's Bob

Smith against SMU in 1950. Smith was in the stands watching Leaks play.

"I don't really keep up that much with records, but he had a pretty long way to go until he got that long run on the last play of the game," Smith said.

Leaks's UT mark was broken by Ricky Williams, who rushed for 350 yards against Iowa State in 1998. TCU's Tony Jeffrey topped his SWC rushing record by one yard against Tulane in 1987.

Promoting the Wishbone Quarterback

During the 1975 season, Marty Akins was one of the best Wishbone quarterbacks in college football and led Texas to a 10-2 record and a 38-21 come-from-behind victory over Colorado in the Bluebonnet Bowl.

UT coach Darrell Royal had a gripe that his Wishbone quarterbacks didn't get the recognition passing quarterbacks got in those days.

"When you are selecting All-Americans, I think you ought to consider the teams that are ranked the highest," Royal said at the time. "I think the All-America selections are influenced by a player's pro [passing] potential. But check the top 10 teams in the country. They're mostly running teams."

After a 41-9 victory over Rice during the 1975 season, Royal said, "Marty [Akins] pitched out on five touchdowns. To me that's like five touchdown passes. And if he had thrown for five touchdown passes, he would be in headlines all over the country."

Loud and Clear

At least some of the members of the Football Writers Association of America (FWAA) were listening to Royal. During its All-America Committee meeting in December 1975, the FWAA did not go along with the Associated Press's first-team selection of UCLA's John Sciarra, a passing quarterback. The committee deliberated for four hours and finally was deadlocked (4-4) between Akins and Sciarra. That prompted committee member Gus Schrader of the *Cedar Rapids Gazette* to telephone Washington coach Don James, who had played both teams that season, losing to Texas (28-10) and beating UCLA (17-13).

"I guess I should be loyal to the Pac-10," James said. "But the truth is whatever we did, Akins made us wrong. And we could handle Sciarra."

The FWAA chose Akins as its All-America quarterback.

Some of the best option quarterbacks of that era had been at UT and Oklahoma. Names such as James Street, Eddie Phillips, and Alan Lowry at Texas; Jack Mildren and Steve Davis at Oklahoma; and Gary Rutledge of Alabama.

CHAPTER SIX

Texas-Oklahoma Series

One of the greatest spectacles in college football occurs at the Cotton Bowl each October when Texas and Oklahoma meet in the Red River Shootout. The game pits two states, two rabid football followings, and more often than not, two nationally ranked teams against each other in a stadium that is equally divided between burnt orange and crimson and red fans.

It's a football series that has been filled with chills, spills, and thrills for more than 70 years at the same neutral site.

"I had the opportunity every year to come up here and play in the Texas-Oklahoma game, and there is no feeling in the world like walking down that chute going into the Cotton Bowl," said former UT quarterback James Street, who beat the Sooners in 1968 (26-20) and 1969 (27-17).

The border game started on campus sites in 1900 with a 28-2 UT victory. It was moved to Dallas from 1912 to 1919, except for 1913 when the game was played in Houston and in 1918 when the two teams didn't play.

After 1919, the series was discontinued until 1922 and was held on campus sites that season and the following year before another five-year interruption.

Since 1929, the game has been played in Fair Park and has become a fixture at the State Fair of Texas.

Inspirational Speech

During the early stages of the UT-Oklahoma game in 1914, UT lineman Louis Jordan was upset after an early Sooner touchdown left Texas trailing, 7-0. He lectured his teammates: "Nobody leaves this field until we beat the hell out of them."

Sure enough, UT did. The Longhorns scored 32 unanswered points and posted a 32-7 victory over the Sooners on the way to an 8-0 season. Eleven UT players started and ended the game.

Later, a flagpole was erected in Jordan's honor. It was donated by his native city of Fredericksburg, Texas, at the dedication of Memorial Stadium in 1924. In 1918, Jordan died in World War I.

Jack Crain: OU Tormentor

Texas's star halfback Jack "Rabbit" Crain was a nightmare for the Sooners from 1939-41.

In 1939, trailing 17-0, UT got two long touchdown runs from Crain, a 160-pound sophomore, to bring the Longhorns to 17-12. Both of his point-after-touchdown attempts were blocked, and OU hung on to win, 24-12.

In 1940, Oklahoma took a 16-7 lead, but wound up losing, 19-16.

Crain was at it again. He dashed 63 yards to set up UT's second score. And after an Oklahoma turnover, he scored the winning touchdown from nine yards out. He then sealed the victory with an interception on OU's ensuing possession.

In 1941, Crain rushed for 144 yards on 10 carries and accounted for two touchdowns and four extra-point conversions in a 40-7 UT triumph.

The UT-OU Hat Tradition

The Golden Hat Trophy is emblematic of victory in the annual Texas-Oklahoma game in Dallas.

The tradition originated in 1941 when a genuine felt 10-gallon cowboy hat was donated by the State Fair of Texas in recognition that the game is played annually at the Cotton Bowl and is a top attraction of the State Fair. Its original value was estimated at $50. In 1941, Texas beat OU 40-7; it was the first time the hat was awarded to the winning team.

The State Fair of Texas originally had the hat bronzed and called it the Bronze Hat. In 1969, the State Fair of Texas had the hat re-plated in gold, and it is now called the Golden Hat.

That caused a small controversy among some of the original creators of the trophy, who wanted the name to be retained as the Bronzed Cowboy Hat or the Cowboy Bronze Hat. The Golden Hat is now kept in the trophy case of the winning team each year.

A Play for Roommates

Rooster Andrews and Bobby Layne became roommates in 1944 when Layne arrived at Texas. Layne woke Rooster up one night while the two were in their dorm room.

Andrews related this story of pillow talk.

"When you are back there drop-kicking on extra points, I wonder if you could fake the thing and you could throw it to me in the left flat?" Layne asked Andrews. "I will fake a block and just go out on the left flat. Your grandson could hit me out on the flat."

Layne called the play in the huddle during a 20-0 victory over OU a few weeks later.

"Coach Bible had seen us practice it the Tuesday before we played Oklahoma," Andrews said. "But he left the play calling all to Bobby. They got together before the game. But he called him Bob. He said, 'Now Bob, you know what my plans are. You just fit in with the way the game is going.' I went out there prepared to drop-kick, and Bob said we are going to pull 'Our Play.'"

It worked.

Royal as an OU Player

Future UT coach Darrell Royal, born in Hollis, Oklahoma, played for the Sooners from 1946 to 1949 and was a standout halfback-quarterback who passed for 509 yards and rushed for 189 more as a senior. He split four games at the Cotton Bowl with UT.

Royal lost games his freshman and sophomore seasons, but as coach Bud Wilkinson's juggernaut began to pick up steam, the Sooners beat Texas by identical scores of 20-14 in 1948 and 1949.

"You think the same thing every year as you come down the runway," said Royal in 1957 when he became the Longhorns' head coach. "Everybody has experienced it, as a coach and as a player. There was a little tingly bubbly feeling. I felt light-headed. It felt like my feet were hardly touching the ramp; my mouth tasted like cotton."

Royal was named an All-American in the 1949 season when Oklahoma went 11-0. Royal also played defense and punted. He had 17 interceptions during his career in Norman. He once had an 81-yard punt and had punt returns of 73 and 95 yards during his career.

And the Bottles Rained on Them

Controversy. That was the theme of third-ranked Texas's victory over Oklahoma during the 1947 season.

When referee Jack Sisco ruled that there was still one second remaining on the first-half clock, it allowed Texas to score a touchdown to go ahead 14-7 on a frantic play when Randall Clay scored after UT had appeared to have fumbled the ball. Clay had come up with it and run into the end zone. OU coach Bud Wilkinson claimed that Clay's knee was on the ground when he retrieved the ball and the touchdown should have been disallowed. But the play stood.

Texas would go on to win 34-14 behind Bobby Layne, whose passing and ball-handling wizardry opened up the game in the second half, but not before another controversy.

OU drew within seven at 21-14. On UT's next drive, Sisco made another controversial call after Darrell Royal intercepted a pass to apparently stall a UT drive. Sisco called OU for unnecessary roughness on Layne after he released the ball. That gave the ball back to Texas.

The Sooners' portion of the Cotton Bowl crowd went crazy. Booze and soda pop bottles and other items came raining onto the Cotton Bowl floor. After order was restored, UT scored to make it 28-14.

"My first reaction was to keep my headgear on and get right smack in the middle," recounted Darrell Royal years later. "If anybody was going to hit me with a Coke bottle, he was going to have to throw it the furthest distance possible."

Texas added another touchdown. After the game, Sisco, along with the other game officials, had to be taken by highway patrol car to safety.

Dizzying Hits

Going into the 1951 game, UT had lost three straight games to OU. But this time the Longhorns prevailed 9-7. The game included one gruesome series of hits early in the fourth quarter, with Oklahoma getting the ball on its two-yard line after Texas saw a 90-yard drive yield nothing.

OU quarterback Eddie Crowder, being rushed by Texas end Paul Williams, back-pedaled to deep in the end zone and just got a pass off to the eventual Heisman Trophy winner the following season, Billy Vessels. As he was releasing the ball, Williams smashed Crowder into the right goalpost and drove it backward. Crowder was dazed, crumpled to the ground, and had to leave the game.

Vessels caught the pass and ran out of the end zone, but he was tackled by guard Harley Sewell and linebackers Don Cunningham and June Davis. Vessels, who left the game with a knee injury, was finished for the season.

But a year later, Crowder and Vessels got their revenge when they helped rout Texas 49-20. It was the first time a team had scored that many points against UT since OU won 50-0 in 1908.

Royal Beats Teacher

In 1958, Texas upset No. 2 Oklahoma 15-14, as the pupil Darrell Royal beat his teacher and former coach, Bud Wilkinson.

But Royal, as reported in *The Dallas Morning News,* apparently had an upset stomach after his first victory over the Sooners as UT coach.

Royal's team had beaten Georgia and Fran Tarkenton, Tulane in UT's 400th victory, and Texas Tech. It was the first time in eight years that both teams came into the game unbeaten.

This was also the first year of the two-point conversion, a new rule introduced to college football. And Royal utilized it on the first touchdown to give UT an 8-0 lead. That turned out to be the winning margin. After the game, Royal said he still didn't like it, although it helped UT win the game. He called it unfair to the coaches.

Quarterback Vince Matthews, a fourth-stringer, directed the Longhorns down the field after OU had gone ahead 14-8. But on third and goal from the seven-yard line, Royal, playing a hunch, inserted Bobby Lackey again for a jump-pass play. Lackey completed the pass to Bobby Bryant for the tying touchdown. He then kicked the extra point to win the game.

It was UT's first victory over Oklahoma since 1951.

Lackey: One-Man Wrecking Crew

In UT's 1958 upset, UT quarterback Bobby Lackey was a defensive star as well. Lackey recovered a fumbled punt on the one-yard line to prevent an OU score. He stopped Bobby Boyd when the Sooners star appeared to be loose for a touchdown with only one minute remaining in the game. Lackey then made a one-handed interception at the UT 28 to save the game.

Beating No. 1

In 1963, Oklahoma came into the game as the No. 1-ranked team in the country. But No. 2 Texas won 28-7.

Oklahoma had upset No. 1 and defending national champion USC earlier in the season. OU's controversial runner, Joe Don Looney, had charged his line was not blocking for him. OU's starting quarterback, Mike Ringer, was out with an elbow injury.

Looney gained only four yards on six carries. UT's defense was solid. And its running game was good enough to beat OU. UT completed only one pass in the game but still won its sixth straight over the Sooners.

"Yeah, we're No. 1 now," Outland Trophy winner Scott Appleton told the press after the game. "We've been No. 1 the last two years, but we let down. This year, we are not going to let down."

Appleton had 18 tackles in the game.

Outland Winners Dominant

From 1958 to 1965, Texas won eight straight games in the series. That also happened from 1940 to 1947, as the Longhorns dominated during the World War II era.

Texas's defense was especially dominating from 1961 to 1965 as two Texas Outland Trophy winners made their presence felt.

Tackle Scott Appleton spearheaded three straight victories from 1961 to 1963, as the Longhorns allowed Oklahoma just 20 points. During linebacker Tommy Nobis's defensive run, the Longhorns allowed only 14 Sooners points in three games from 1963 to 1965.

"Scott was more of a finesse guy—not that he wouldn't put a hit on you," said David McWilliams, who was Appleton's roommate. "But he would slip blocks, jump this way and jump back in, and completely get free and make a tackle. Nobis would just knock the blocker down."

In UT's 28-7 victory over Oklahoma in 1964, Nobis had 25 tackles.

Ending the Streak

In 1966, Oklahoma's Mike Vachon, a sophomore from Amarillo, Texas, kicked four field goals (31, 43, 20, 41 yards) to lead OU to an 18-9 victory and end UT's eight-game winning streak in the series. But it would merely put a patch on the bloodletting. Texas would win four straight in the OU series after this game.

Still, it was the first time in 28 years any OU player had kicked a field goal against Texas at the Cotton Bowl.

OU coach Jim Mackenzie, in his only appearance in the game before his death after the season, decided to pass against the Longhorns. He unleashed quarterback Bob Warmack, who completed 12 of 21 passes for 220 yards against Texas.

The Sooners came out in red helmets with an OU logo after wearing white helmets for 20 years.

Defensively Speaking

Heisman Trophy winner Steve Owens was 0-3 against UT from 1967to 1969. The Sooners running back ran for more than 100 yards in the first two losses. And he happened to break Gale Sayers's Big Eight career rushing mark in his final loss to UT 27-17 in 1969.

But he never really went crazy against Texas, running the ball as he often did against OU opponents in those days.

During the 1968 game won by the Longhorns 26-20, UT defensive tackle Lloyd Wainscott downed a punt on the one-yard line, tackled the quarterback in the end zone for a safety, stripped the ball from the quarterback to set up another touchdown, and recorded 18 tackles.

Wishbone Gets Started

UT's famed Wishbone was still in its infancy stages for the 1968 game versus Oklahoma. The Longhorns had only a 1-1-1 record and were unranked going into the game. But they prevailed 26-20 with some dramatic fourth-quarter heroics.

UT fullback Steve Worster was the workhorse, with 121 yards rushing on 14 carries. His late touchdown was the difference in the game. But UT quarterback James Street was an effective passer on the final drive and finished with 144 yards passing.

Royal's Last Texas-OU Game

It was the intriguing 1976 "Spy Game," which ended in a 6-6 tie. This was an especially bitter game.

While Royal's UT teams from 1958 to 1970 won 12 of 13 games in the OU series, this tie meant Royal was winless (0-5-1) in his last six Texas-OU games. He retired at the end of the 1976 season.

Two days before the game, Royal accused the Sooners of spying on UT practices. Reporter Robert Heard quoted Royal calling OU coach Barry Switzer and his assistant coaches "dirty bastards." Royal offered Switzer and the alleged spy, Lonnie Williams, $10,000 each if they could pass a polygraph test.

Williams, who was living in the Dallas area, had coached with OU defensive coordinator Larry Lacewell at Wichita State. But both Switzer and Lacewell denied the charges. Years later, Lacewell admitted to Royal that the spying charges were true.

But at the time, it just made feelings boil between the rivals in a brutally hard-hitting game.

UT appeared to be on its way to a 6-0 victory. The Longhorns, however, fumbled at their own 37 with 5:23 remaining. OU's Horace Ivory scored from the one with 1:38 to play to tie the score, but a high snap never allowed OU kicker Uwe von Schamann a chance to kick. A hurried pass was intercepted by UT's Steve Collier in the end zone. And the game ended in a tie.

"It was weird," said David McWilliams, a UT assistant coach at the time. "It was like the twilight zone."

Campbell's Breakthrough vs. OU

During Heisman Trophy winner Earl Campbell's career, Texas was 1-2-1 against the Sooners from 1974 to 1977.

Campbell failed to gain 100 yards rushing in his first three games against OU. And Texas lost twice in 1974 and 1975 and tied the Sooners 6-6 in 1976.

Campbell, the Heisman Trophy winner his senior season, finally went over the century mark rushing in the final game of the series in 1977 when Texas beat No. 2 Oklahoma 13-6. He carried 23 times for 124 yards and a touchdown (a 24-yard sprint draw before halftime.)

"Unbelievable," Switzer said of Campbell. "I told him I hope he wins the Heisman Trophy. Our people haven't had the chance to see him like the coaches saw him in the past three years. When you get down to Campbell and one defensive guy, it's impossible."

Akers's Favorite Campbell Play

UT coach Fred Akers remembers that longest wasn't always best for Earl Campbell.

"My favorite play was right in front of OU's bench in the 1977 game," said Akers, who was in his first season as UT's head coach. "I think every defender hit him twice on the same play. It was a seven-yard gain. And he twisted and turned and was hit and came back off of it so many times. Then the official made a mistake and thought he was down and he wasn't. He came out of it and they blew the play dead. It was a great run. Some of his very best runs were from four to 10 yards."

Akers-Switzer Relationship

With Fred Akers becoming the Texas coach in 1977, the dynamics of the series changed somewhat. No longer was it a bitter feud between the two head coaches.

Akers played running back, quarterback, and defensive back and did some punting and kicking at Arkansas as a collegian. Switzer was a center on the same college team. And Akers stayed a season, along with Switzer as a graduate assistant on the Arkansas football staff.

"I wanted to beat Barry's butt," Akers said. "People used to ask a lot about it. There was a big thing between Barry and Darrell. It was kind of out in the open. I would tell people [Barry] is not in my will. But I like him all right."

Akers Nearly a Sooners Coach

Akers tells the story of how he and Switzer almost wound up on the same Oklahoma coaching staff of Jim Mackenzie in 1966.

Akers was coaching at Lubbock High School when he got his first call from Texas.

"At that time Jim Pittman, assistant coach at Texas, had gotten the head job at Tulane," Akers said. "So there was a position open; [Texas's defensive coordinator] Mike Campbell was recruiting out in Lubbock. He would come over to my house and we would watch football all night. Darrell Royal wanted to go to two wide receivers. They were going to open things up."

Campbell recommended Akers, who was running a wide-open offense at Lubbock High School. Royal offered and Akers accepted the job.

Two days later Akers got a call from Switzer, who was still on the Arkansas staff as an assistant. Arkansas had won the Southwest Conference in 1965 and was preparing to play in the Cotton Bowl.

Switzer told Akers, "Hey, I can't talk about this, because it is not going to be announced until January 2. [Arkansas's defensive coordinator] Jim Mackenzie had taken the Oklahoma job and I am going with him. He wants you to come coach the backs."

"I said, 'Gosh, Barry, I just accepted the job at Texas.'

"He said: 'Well, tell them you can't go.'

"I said, 'I can't do that.'"

And he didn't. Akers went on to Texas. Switzer went on to Oklahoma, and both eventually became head coaches at those schools.

Third-Stringer Prevails for UT

Texas had gone without a victory in the OU series for six seasons from 1971 to 1976. And in 1977, UT coach Fred Akers was down to his third-string quarterback, Randy McEachern, in the first quarter at the Cotton Bowl.

McEachern settled the Longhorns down and led them to an 80-yard scoring drive right before halftime. Coming off a knee injury himself the previous season, McEachern didn't make any mistakes, making sure that Earl Campbell got the ball.

A UT legend was born. After UT's 13-6 victory over Oklahoma, McEachern was carried off the field by his teammates.

"I wouldn't say we got down to him," Akers said. "I would say we discovered him. Two minutes gone in the game, we lost our starter Mark McBath, who was really developing into a top college quarterback. He could run, could throw and was very smart. All our quarterbacks were very intelligent. He broke his ankle. Our No. 2 quarterback, Jon Aune, was a good quarterback. He just hadn't had a chance to prove it."

Before the first quarter was over, however, Aune was gone, too.

"He went back to pass, and without anyone hitting him, his knee gave way," Akers said of Aune's torn knee ligaments. "It was a bad injury. He didn't play again for a year and a half. Half of the fans in the stadium were dead silent. Really no one knew who we would put in. Even the players didn't know. Randy McEachern did one of the best jobs coming to aid a football team. He came to lead."

Texas-OU Ticket Selling in the 1970s

The Texas-OU game was a hot commodity in the 1970s, much as it is today. And tickets to the game were a hot commodity particularly in Oklahoma—available UT players' tickets, that is. During that era, players received complimentary tickets to games. To cut out abuses of ticket selling by players, there are now pass lists.

"Oklahoma players could get more for tickets than Texas players could," former Oklahoma coach Barry Switzer said. "The Texas players would collect tickets and bring them to Oklahoma players. They would meet. And Oklahoma players would sell their tickets. We were getting $200 apiece, and they were only getting $50 down there. They knew where the market was. Players talk. Hell, yeah, our players would do it for them. We were winning then."

A Judge's Order: Stop the Cable

Bill Little, longtime UT sports publicist, remembers his wackiest trip through the usual bumper-to-bumper traffic to the Cotton Bowl for the annual border war. It occurred when he was following the Dallas sheriff's car into Fair Park.

"We had to get an injunction from federal court in Dallas and get it signed by a judge," Little recalls of stopping a cable telecast of the Texas-OU game into the state of Oklahoma. "We got the injunction—15 minutes before the game started, the judge signed it. And I was following the sheriff's car down Commerce in my old, gray Cadillac to serve the injunction."

In those days before 1984, the NCAA controlled college football television. But games outside the NCAA package still could be telecast into the home markets of the schools—in this case,

Oklahoma City-Norman, Austin, and Dallas. But an Oklahoma City station was showing it on cable throughout the state of Oklahoma. Because it was Texas's designated home game, Texas could be in violation of NCAA rules if the cable plug was not pulled.

"We got it taken off," Little said.

Mack Brown's Most Memorable UT-OU Moment

It came in 1984 when the Longhorns and Sooners went into the game as the No.1- and No. 3-ranked teams in the country, respectively. Brown was an assistant coach for Barry Switzer's Sooners.

Brown said the Oklahoma team busses drove into the Stare Fair of Texas before the game in a pouring rain. The two powerhouses battled to a 15-15 tie.

"You couldn't see on either side, and in the old days you drove right down the middle of the fairgrounds," Brown said. "... And I have never seen that many people in the rain screaming at each other. It was the most unbelievable thing.... And it rained so hard you couldn't see throughout the game. And not one person left the stadium. I just wasn't used to that. There is usually a TV in a bar somewhere that somebody would go watch. That told me how special this game was back then."

OU Steaming Mad in 1984

The 1984 Texas-Oklahoma game ended in a 15-15 tie on a series of controversial calls, which allowed Texas to tie the score as time was running out. After OU had taken a safety on purpose for a 15-12 lead, UT got the ball at its 44 with 2:10 remaining in the game.

On UT's last-gasp drive, Oklahoma appeared to have recovered a fumble on a hit by OU linebacker Paul Migliazzo. OU's Tony Casillas fell on the ball, but officials ruled the UT player was already down when he fumbled.

OU partisans were not happy.

After a controversial defensive pass interference call gave UT a first down at the OU 41, Texas worked its way down the field. UT quarterback Todd Dodge then tried to find a receiver in the right corner of the end zone, but a wobbly pass went through the hands of an OU defender and into the hands of another, Keith Stanberry.

Stanberry was ruled out of bounds by officials. But television replays showed that he was in bounds.

"I thought we had the game won when Texas fumbled and we recovered early on the last drive," Switzer said. "It was right in front of me and I saw the ball come flying out when the Texas player was hit. But a Southwest Conference official took it away from us. [Stanberry's disallowed interception was] another play they took away from us."

"As time expired, Barry Switzer was running right by me, chasing the officials," UT kicker Jeff Ward said.

Ward's Ingenuity

Despite the protests from OU, Texas had the ball in a position to tie the score, and the Longhorns did. Jeff Ward kicked a 32-yard field goal as time ran out for the 15-15 tie during a rainy day.

"We probably had 30 balls and we ran out of dry ones," Ward said. "The line judge will throw a ball to the umpire, who will set the ball [at the line of scrimmage]. A lot of times they drop in the water. I don't know how many times I had to go back to an official and ask for another ball. Kicking isn't the problem. It's finding a dry ball."

Right before the game-tying kick, Ward's holder, Rob Moerschell, said, "My hands are soaking wet and I don't have a dry towel."

Ward grabbed one from an official before making the kick despite a high snap.

"I went to Moerschell in the locker room and told him he did a good job," Ward said. "But the ball felt like it weighed 12 pounds. He had kept the ball, which was stamped Oklahoma. I can never call Barry Switzer dumb."

The 1985 Game: Defensive Struggle

In 1985, Oklahoma won 14-7 in a defensive struggle. OU quarterback Troy Aikman, the future Dallas Cowboys All-Pro who would later transfer to UCLA to complete his college eligibility, completed four of nine passes and was sacked three times. Texas was held to 70 yards total offense, 53 passing and 17 yards rushing.

"It was the greatest defensive performance ever by an Oklahoma team since I have been here," Oklahoma coach Barry Switzer said. "And that's 20 years."

Questioning the Dallas Site

Before the 1987 Texas-Oklahoma game in Dallas, Oklahoma coach Barry Switzer suggested that the game be moved to campus sites. Switzer was unhappy with the coverage OU was getting from the Dallas media, including probes by *The Dallas Morning News* into alleged improprieties in the OU program during that era.

"It was the Dallas press," Switzer said.

"They treated us like a bastard son. We came down there every year and it wasn't neutral. It never will be. It was a rehash of my deal or some deal or something negative every year.... We got tired of that."

But Switzer said the game should remain in Dallas, where it has been played since 1929. UT officials and coaches have never suggested that the game should be moved to campus sites.

"The tradition and all would change," Switzer said.

"A home-and-home would be like a home-and-home with Nebraska. You'd get 5,000 seats when we went up there. They would get 5,000 seats when they came down here. There is no influx of monies into the state. Texas is going to stay there in Dallas."

Peter the Great

From 1989 to 1992, UT quarterback Peter Gardere of Texas would start four games and go 4-0 against the Sooners in a series of close and dramatic games. He received the nickname "Peter the Great" for those performances.

"The year before, I can remember [another quarterback] Shannon Kelley stopping me in the dorm and telling me that if you play or start in any game, make sure it is the OU game," said Gardere, who was a redshirt in 1988 and traveled to Dallas with the team. "I had played in every game [during the 1989 season] up until the OU game. The Rice game was my first start. I was just excited to get into a game."

Any reason why Gardere played so well against Oklahoma? He said the week before the 1988 OU game he had to quarterback the option as part of the scout team and was beaten up in practice.

"And in the locker room, the whole week of the OU game, the OU fight song is playing," Gardere said. "You were so sick of it before the game. You were tired of hearing it."

Those Winning Passes

In 1989, Texas came from behind to beat OU 28-24. Texas had not beaten OU since the 1983 season and had blown a 21-7 halftime lead. The Longhorns trailed 24-21 with little more than three minutes remaining in the game.

Gardere completed four straight passes to put the Longhorns in a position to win. On the fifth pass, Gardere found Johnny Walker from 25 yards out with 1:33 remaining to win the game 28-24.

"On the pass to Johnny Walker, they brought a safety blitz," Gardere said. "The guy was five feet from me when I let the ball go. I threw it up. And Johnny made a great catch. He got up and got it. It was a great play."

A year later it was very much the same story as Texas knocked off No. 4 Oklahoma 14-13. Gardere led the Longhorns to the OU 16. From there, on fourth and seven, Gardere found Keith Cash in the end zone for the winning touchdown with two minutes remaining.

"The Cash play was the exact same play we ran to Johnny Walker the year before," Gardere said. "We knew the defense would be playing towards Johnny. And we went the other way to Keith. So it worked."

Quarterback Peter Gardere started—and won—four straight
games against Oklahoma from 1989 to 1992.
Cotton Bowl Athletic Association

A Foot to Spare

In the 1994 game, it took a gallant goal-line stand by the No.
15 Longhorns to preserve a 17-10 victory over the No. 16 Sooners.

On OU's fourth-and-goal play from the three in the final
seconds, UT's 343-pound noseguard Stonie Clark made a stop on
OU running back James Allen at the one-yard line. It was actually at
about the one-foot line.

OU quarterback Garrick McGee took the snap and ran right,
looking as if he had handed off behind the right tackle. But Allen
crossed behind McGee, took the handoff and headed around the left
end. UT's Robert Reed turned him inside where Clark waited.

"Fourth-down plays, you always see them on TV," Clark said after the game. "You just want to make one yourself. That's why I play college football."

Strange Play Call

In the 24-24 tie during the 1995 season, UT coach John Mackovic made one of the strangest calls of his career during the final 10 minutes of the game. Instead of going for the go-ahead field goal, which would have put Texas ahead 27-24, Mackovic elected to run Ricky Williams wide on a fourth-and-one play.

Williams was stopped for a six-yard loss when he was tackled by OU cornerback Larry Bush almost immediately in the backfield. The play was called Option Left but had worked better when quarterback James Brown ran it.

OU's head coach Howard Schnellenberger said OU assistant coaches had analyzed UT's tendencies in such situations and made the call.

"I thought we could get outside quicker than them," Mackovic said after the game. "When we came back to the line, they'd switched defenses, and the cornerback was not as tight. We had a great setup. We thought we could run. Sometimes those plays go untouched. We felt if we got a touchdown, it would put pressure on them."

Instead, Texas got nothing, and the game ended in a 24-24 tie.

Allen's Redemption

In 1996, James Allen's two-yard run beat Texas 30-27 in overtime. Allen had his revenge for the 1994 loss when he was stopped short of the goal line in a 17-10 Sooners loss.

Allen rushed for 159 yards on 23 carries. He gained 112 of those yards in the second half when Oklahoma rallied from a 24-13 deficit to tie the score 27-27 with 2:26 left in the game.

"When it is cloudy out there, you just wait for the sun to come out," Allen said.

The 1996 game produced the first overtime in UT history. OU coach John Blake wept as he left the field. OU was a 22-point underdog going into the game.

Williams vs. Parker

The 1997 Texas-Oklahoma game turned into a rushing duel between UT running back Ricky Williams and his counterpart at OU, De'Mond Parker.

Williams carried the ball 40 times (second highest number of carries in his career) for 223 yards and two touchdowns.

It was the first time a UT back had gone over 100 yards rushing against Oklahoma since Edwin Simmons rushed 14 times for 100 yards in 1983.

Parker rushed for 291 yards on 31 carries and scored three touchdowns, but UT prevailed 27-24.

"The biggest thing for our offensive line was that it was able to get right up on top of everybody and give Ricky some running room," UT coach John Mackovic said. "Today we were solid when we were running right at them."

Miniature UT Winning Streak

As Oklahoma's program floundered in the mid- to late 1990s under John Blake, before Bob Stoops got it turned around, UT won three straight games against the outmanned Sooners from 1997 to 1999.

Coach John Mackovic's last UT team beat Oklahoma 27-24 during a 4-7 season. And Mack Brown's first two UT teams registered 34-3 and 38-28 victories during the 1998 and 1999 seasons, respectively.

After the 1999 victory, Brown presented former UT coach Darrell Royal with the game ball after the game during a very touching and emotional moment in the UT locker room.

In the 1998 victory, Heisman Trophy winner Ricky Williams donned Doak Walker's No. 37 in a moving tribute to the former SMU runner who graced the gridiron of the Cotton Bowl a half-century before. Williams won the Doak Walker National Running Back Award in 1997 and 1998.

"I knew I didn't want to embarrass myself wearing Doak's number," said Williams of the deceased great. He didn't. Williams rushed for 139 yards on 31 carries.

Series Record—Wrong Way

Scoring the most points in a series game, Oklahoma scored the first five times it had the ball on the way to a 63-14 victory over Texas in the 2000 game. Oklahoma had a 42-0 lead before Texas could even score in the second quarter.

This game did nothing to quiet the broiling quarterback controversy at Texas between starter Major Applewhite and backup Chris Simms. Both were equally ineffective.

Blevins Recounts Coaches' Wishes

Oklahoma sportscaster Dean Blevins whispered to a reporter during the closing minutes of Oklahoma's 14-3 victory over Texas in 2001.

"The OU coaches were praying they didn't put in Major Applewhite," Blevins said.

Bob Stoops's prayers were answered. The Longhorns coaching staff didn't play Applewhite, the senior quarterback reserve.

OU coaches feared the gutsy Applewhite more than the rather predictable Simms, whose mobility is not as good as Applewhite's. Sure enough, Blevins hardly had the words out of his mouth when a Simms miscue near the goal line turned into the clinching touchdown with just more than two minutes remaining in the game.

OU safety Roy Williams hit Simms's arm, and his pass fluttered in the air and into the hands of OU linebacker Teddy Lehman, who literally walked in for the score.

The Tunnel Problem

The Texas-Oklahoma postgame news conferences, often held in the tunnel or a room off to the side, finally ended after the 2000 game. With the help of the UT sports information office's John Bianco and Scott McConnell and the Cotton Bowl's Charlie Fiss, a tent was set up behind the State Fair administration building starting with OU's 14-3 victory in 2001.

This also ended the tradition of the bands leaving the stadium up the tunnel and the winning team's band playing. Because the area has been barricaded off to exit the stadium, the bands now have to disperse through the stands.

Thus ended some of the most frightening and crowded news conferences on record, with bands blaring either "Boomer Sooner" or the "Eyes of Texas" and coaches trying to talk and players covering their ears.

One year, two employees (one from *The Dallas Morning News* and the other from WFAA-TV) from Dallas-based Belo Corporation nearly came to blows because they were fighting for space in the tiny interview room. One reporter had his foot run over in the tunnel by a golf cart.

Another OU Victory

Oklahoma rallied to win the 2002 game in the second half 35-24.

Texas held a 14-3 lead near the end of the first half. But Oklahoma scored a touchdown with five seconds remaining in the first half and added a two-point conversion pass, which reduced UT's lead to 14-11.

That seemed to swing the momentum of the game toward the Sooners.

Oklahoma used a 21-point fourth quarter to win its third straight in the series. UT quarterback Chris Simms failed to beat OU during his career when he was intercepted three times, sacked four times, and failed to throw a touchdown pass.

Simms did have two one-yard runs for touchdowns, but had minus-18 rushing yards.

"Oklahoma did what great teams do," said UT cornerback Rod Barbers. "They got momentum back on their side. They didn't panic."

Interception Bowl

UT quarterback Chris Simms threw three interceptions in 2002 against OU, a game that OU won 35-24. In three appearances against OU (2000-2002), Simms finished with eight interceptions and was on the losing side each time.

When a Dallas television reporter asked Simms after the 2002 game why he had trouble winning big games, coach Mack Brown interceded.

"Of course, it's disappointing," Simms said later in the news conference. "I don't know if anyone in this room wanted to win this game more than me."

Texas Sees Sooner Magic

In the 2002 UT-OU game, Oklahoma coach Bob Stoops ran his record to 9-1 in games against top-10 ranked teams with the 35-24 victory over Texas. Maybe it takes some breaks to win the big games. Certainly, Oklahoma received one when wide receiver Will Peoples fumbled near the goal line and running back Quentin Griffin scooped it up and scored early in the fourth quarter to give OU a 21-17 lead.

"I'll take all the Sooner Magic I can get," Stoops said. "We'll sprinkle some here and sprinkle some there. Whether it's good fortune or Sooner Magic, we'll take it either way."

Red River: Judgment Day

The 2003 annual Red River Rivalry in Dallas offered no relief for Texas, which had disposed of Rice, Tulane, and a solid Kansas State team in three games since the upset loss to Arkansas.

The Longhorns entered the 2003 OU game with a quarterback controversy brewing between veteran Chance Mock and freshman Vince Young. And the turnover-filled game (three UT interceptions, three UT fumbles lost) did nothing to really resolve it as the Sooners prevailed 65-13.

Mock, the UT starter, suffered an early interception. And Young had an early fumble near the goal line, with the score 14-7 in favor of top-ranked Oklahoma. Young's fumble seemed to take the life out of the Longhorns, who dropped their fourth straight to the Sooners.

Before the 2005 OU-Texas game, Brown was philosophical about being judged by one game.

"It doesn't really matter," said Brown, whose Longhorns were shut out in the 2004 game 12-0 by the Sooners. "It bothered me four or five years ago. And I get judged on different things by different people. And if this is the one they are judging me on, I haven't done very good. You don't need motivation to coach in any game, especially this one. I wish they would judge me by some of the ones we won all the time."

Bevo Comes to Dallas

It has become a UT tradition that Bevo arrives on the front lawn of Ken and Laura Capps' house near Lovers Lane each Thursday before the annual Texas-Oklahoma game at the Cotton Bowl.

Bevo No. 14 started the trek with the 2004 game and eventually brought home a Rose Bowl winner in his first season. In 2005, Bevo No. 14 , which will turn three in March 2006, had put on considerable weight and was at 1,500 pounds.

Bevo No. 13 was retired after the 2003 season after 16 years of service.

"[No. 14] was young last year," said Garrett Godwin, one of four Silver Spur handlers. "But he has a lot of growing room. He is like Shaquille O'Neal when he was playing basketball in the seventh grade."

Godwin said Bevo. No. 14 has the potential to weigh between 2,000 and 2,500 pounds and have record-length horns, spreading 100 inches. He could be in service for two decades.

Ghosts of Texas Past Put to Rest

From 2000 to 2004 , the Cotton Bowl and the second Saturday in October have been a chamber of horrors for Texas. In 2005, that changed when the Longhorns beat OU 45-12 in the 100th game of the series.

"It feels better than I thought it would," said UT's senior tight end David Thomas. "A lot better."

The Longhorns scored more points on Oklahoma than at any time in history. And the 33-point victory over the Sooners tied for UT's most decisive in history (40-7 in 1941) over Oklahoma.

Texas coach Mack Brown seemed to want and stay and ride some of the rides on the nearby Texas State Fair midway, he was so pumped about the day and the future. His second-ranked Longhorns moved to 5-0 with the victory over the Sooners.

"Yes, the emotions you have are for the fans," said Brown, who is 3-5 overall against OU through the 2005 season. "They are the ones who have suffered through this series lately. And your emotions are for your players. They've accomplished a lot but haven't gotten recognition nationally because of this game."

The Longhorns' knockout punches to the Sooners were three first-half touchdowns, two of them on single plays: an 80-yard run by freshman tailback Jamaal Charles and a 64-yard pass from UT quarterback Vincent Young to Billy Pittman right before halftime.

The Longhorns also added a first-half field goal for a solid 24-6 lead.

Brown's pregame speech?

"It was very similar to Ohio State," Brown said. "Let's enjoy it and do the things we have to do to win today. But let's not let it get bigger than it is."

Young's Stadium Celebration Finally at Cotton Bowl

After UT's 2005 victory over Oklahoma, Young ran over to the Texas sections of Cotton Bowl and patted the hands of Longhorns fans lining the front rows. It was his first victory after two previous losses to the Sooners in Dallas.

"The fans deserve it, staying with us," Young said. "I wanted to touch their hands, so they know we appreciate what they are."

Texas quarterback Vince Young takes the ball and runs during the Texas Longhorns' 45-12 win over the Oklahoma Sooners. *James D. Smith/Icon SMI*

Mack Brown added about Young, who threw three touchdown passes: "He played as good a game at the line of scrimmage as I have seen him play."

Oklahoma was intent on trying to bottle up Young at the line of scrimmage. But he went to the passing game, completing five straight passes in the opening scoring drive, which set the tone for the day.

Young passed for 241 yards (completing 14 of 27 passes) against OU and rushed for 45 yards and had no turnovers. It was by far Young's best day at the Cotton Bowl.

"Sure, it's obvious," Oklahoma coach Bob Stoops said of Young's improvement. "The longer he is out there the more experience he has and the easier he sees things."

Brown left Young in the entire game, even with UT ahead 45-12 late in the fourth quarter.

"I wanted Vince to enjoy it," Brown said. "I wanted him to be out there at the end of the game. Right or wrong, we thought he had earned the right."

Charles Is Fearless

UT's freshman running back Jamaal Charles appears to like the big game settings. He had a nice receiving game at Ohio State and gained 116 yards rushing on nine carries against Oklahoma, boosted mostly by an explosive 13-second 80-yard touchdown run in the second quarter.

"He has tremendous speed, and he can jump sideways," UT coach Mack Brown said. "He doesn't seem to be bothered by the environments of big games like this and Ohio State."

Charles got some advice from UT quarterback Vince Young.

"I told him to use his speed," Young said. "His speed is faster than game speed."

Through five games of the 2005 season, Charles already had 563 rushing yards, which ranked as the eighth-best single-season total in UT history among Longhorns freshmen. He was in reach of Cedric Benson's freshman record of 1,053 yards in 2001.

Rod Wright's Play Worthy of ESPN

Before the 100th Texas-Oklahoma game, UT's six-foot-five, 315-pound senior defensive tackle Rod Wright envisioned what it would be like if ESPN played highlights of a Texas's domination of OU.

Wright didn't know he would provide a personal highlight in the fourth quarter when he returned OU quarterback Rhett Bomar's fumble 67 yards for the game's final score.

"It happened so fast I was in denial the whole time I was running and the whole time I was celebrating in the end zone," Wright said. "I was tired. It hadn't sunk in."

He added: "I was on the team which lost to them 65-13 [in 2003]. They knew we would play to the end. And we knew they would play to the end."

CHAPTER SEVEN

Cotton Memories

Through the 2004 season, Texas had participated in 22 Cotton Bowl games, more than any other team.

The Longhorns missed the first six Cotton Bowls. Then they claimed back-to-back Southwest Conference championships during the 1942 and 1943 seasons and became frequent visitors to Dallas's New Year's Day Classic.

At one point, the Longhorns won six straight SWC titles and qualified for Cotton Bowls from 1969 to 1974. Through the 2002 season, Texas has an 11-10-1 record in Cotton Bowl games.

Going Bowling

In the 1943 Classic, the Longhorns beat Georgia Tech 14-7 before 36,000 fans. But Texas had to make a goal-line stand led by tackle Stan Mauldin in the fourth quarter to hand Georgia Tech its first bowl defeat.

A year later, Texas returned to the 1944 Cotton Bowl and tied military team Randolph Field 7-7 in a defensive struggle. A cold, rainy day was the worst Texas coach D.X. Bible said he had endured in 30 years of coaching. It was the first and only time a military installation played in the Cotton Bowl.

A Cotton Bowl Party

In the 1946 Cotton Bowl game, UT's Bobby Layne put on a dazzling performance in the Longhorns' 40-27 victory over Missouri. Layne completed 11 of 12 passes, scored four touchdowns and had a hand in all 40 points. UT's All-America end Hub Bechtol caught nine passes for 138 yards.

That's not to say the Tigers from Ol' Mizzou were pushovers.

Texas's defense had been nearly impenetrable in the Southwest Conference that season, allowing only 421 yards in six games and no more than two touchdowns to any SWC opponent.

Missouri gained 408 yards rushing and 106 yards passing in a highly entertaining game. But the game was probably no more entertaining than the night before.

"A bunch of these Missouri guys had been on these All-Star squads," said Rooster Andrews, Layne's roommate. "And they were all good friends of mine. They were good guys. That was the night before the Cotton Bowl. And we went over to where they were staying. We enjoyed some beverages. We stayed up pretty late because I knew Bobby [Layne] could stand it. It was Bobby's way of thinking, let's entertain them royally. Let's see how late we can keep them up.

"I'll tell you who thought he was tougher than Layne, and that was Jim Kekeris [a 284-pound tackle]. He kept needling Bobby that night. After about three or four beers, he said, 'I'll show you tomorrow.'

"Bobby said, 'OK, Jim, we will see you tomorrow.'"

Halftime Advice from General Neyland

Tennessee's sophomore fullback Andy Kozar remembers the halftime scene at the 1951 Cotton Bowl. General Robert Neyland, the coach of the Volunteers, was from Greenville, Texas, and wanted to beat the Longhorns.

"It was 14-7 at halftime, we were behind,' Kozar recalled. "He did not say a word to any of us. Then, with five to seven minutes before the second half started, we went out on the field, and he told us collectively, 'We have been physically whipped in the first half.

But they will be tired in the second half. They outweigh us 20 pounds a man [by average]. You will outlast them. They are going to drop the ball and they will throw it and we intercept it. Now we will all laugh—ha-ha-ha.'

"It started that way and broke into a roar," Kozar said. "He wanted a signal when the Texas team was coming out and they heard us laughing."

With the psyche job, Tennessee wound up winning 20-14, by scoring 13 points in the fourth quarter.

Another Hangover

In the 1951 Cotton Bowl game, No. 4 Tennessee beat No. 3 Texas 20-14 in coach Blair Cherry's final game as the Longhorns' coach. It was Cherry's sixth straight loss against any opponent at the Cotton Bowl Stadium.

Tennessee's sophomore fullback, Andy Kozar, scored the winning touchdown for Tennessee with barely more than three minutes remaining. A lighter Tennessee team, using the single wing of General Bob Neyland, rushed for 295 yards against the favored Longhorns, who obviously didn't take the Volunteers seriously.

Most of the Texas players had attended a New Year's Eve party the night before and didn't get to bed before 2 a.m. It showed in the fourth quarter when Tennessee outscored Texas 13-0 to win the game.

UT quarterback Ben Tompkins still celebrated that evening. He was married to Miss Peggy Webb of Fort Worth, a University of Texas cheerleader.

Reversing the Trend

The 1953 Texas-Tennessee Cotton Bowl game was much different than its predecessor in 1951.

This time around, Texas's defense was prepared for the single wing. Neither Andy Kozar nor General Bob Neyland was a factor in Texas's 16-0 victory. Kozar was out with a back injury, and Neyland was so ill he had turned over the direction of the team to an assistant coach.

How dominant was No. 10 Texas's defense?

No. 8 Tennessee touched the ball on offense just twice in the first quarter and fumbled both times. And once in the second quarter, Texas's defense and a penalty made it fourth and 43 for Tennessee.

Eight members of the UT team had been named All-SWC during the regular season, including running back Dick Ochoa, who was named the most outstanding back. He rushed 26 times for 108 yards despite pulled muscles in both legs.

UT coach Ed Price made sure there was no reoccurrence of partying the night before the game (which hampered UT's performance in 1951). Price secured first-run movies and showed them to the players at the hotel each night. There was a 10 p.m. curfew. And just in case, there were guards at the fire escapes.

Angry Fan

Before the 1953 Cotton Bowl game, in which All-American Harley Sewell was named the outstanding lineman, an angry UT alum called UT assistant coach J.T. King complaining that Sewell was dipping snuff. He wanted to know how King was going to discipline Sewell.

King finally told the alum he needed to do some checking.

"If you'll find out what brand Harley's dipping, I'll recommend it to the whole damn team," King said.

Near Riot

In the 1960 game, Texas was involved in a near riot during Coach Royal's first trip as a head coach to the Cotton Bowl Classic. Syracuse defeated the Longhorns 23-14. The Orangemen entered the game as the national champion and heavy favorite, but Texas showed little respect for the Eastern power.

In the second quarter, tempers got out of control and a brawl nearly occurred. Both teams accused each other of dirty play after the game.

Although Syracuse's Ernie Davis had pulled a hamstring several days before the game, the future Heisman Trophy winner was on the end of an 87-yard touchdown option pass from running back Ger Schwedes early in the game. Davis also scored on a one-yard run and caught two conversion passes.

Syracuse, finishing with an 11-0 record, built up a 15-0 lead, and Texas couldn't catch the Orangemen.

Defensive Struggle

The 1962 Cotton Bowl Classic was a defensive struggle as No. 3 Texas posted a 12-7 victory over No. 5 Ole Miss. It was the Rebels' first loss to a Southwest Conference team in a bowl game.

UT's Jerry Cook intercepted three passes against an Ole Miss team that was ranked second nationally in passing.

"We tried to pick off everything they threw," Cook said. "We felt we had to stop the passes to beat 'em. I guess we surprised them by doing so well with just a three-deep defense, but our line kept the pressure on them."

Another defensive back, safety Duke Carlisle, broke up three passes in the game. But the real defensive star was end Bob Moses, who made two stirring defensive plays.

Early in the third quarter after Texas had thrown a pass interception, Ole Miss was moving in for a potential score. But Moses made a hit on the Ole Miss quarterback on fourth down at the UT 36 to stall the drive. In the fourth quarter, Moses made a game-saving tackle on fourth and two at the Texas 23.

A Year Later

In the 1963 Cotton Bowl Classic, LSU posted a 13-0 victory over the Longhorns when quarterbacks Lynn Amedee and Jimmy Field unleashed a passing attack on UT.

"The complicated defenses that Texas was throwing at us forced us to throw the ball more," LSU coach Charlie McClendon said. "Our reverse away from motion was our most consistently successful running play because their linebackers were going with the motion."

Letter Writing

UT linebacker Johnny Treadwell routinely would psyche himself by getting mad at opponents a couple of days before games. He also would write letters to teammates before games to try to fire them up as well.

Before UT's 13-0 loss to LSU in the 1963 Cotton Bowl Classic, Treadwell allegedly sent a letter to UT co-captain Perry McWilliams with the signature of Fred Miller, LSU's standout tackle.

"I am a Chinese Bandit," the letter read. "You just go ahead and take it easy in practice, have a good time. Don't hit hard and don't go all out, and we will be there in Dallas to humiliate you and your teammates before 75,000 people watching at the Cotton Bowl and millions more watching on TV."

LSU won, but Treadwell psyched himself. He was named the Defensive MVP of the game when he recorded 12 tackles, two for minus-six yards. He also broke up a pass.

Spending Money

Texas's Duke Carlisle, playing in the defensive backfield, found a 50-cent piece on the field of the Cotton Bowl during LSU's 13-0 victory in the 1963 Classic.

"I picked up a 50-cent piece off the ground," Carlisle said. "I thought it was about the only good thing that had happened that day. I stuck it in my pants."

Shortly thereafter, Carlisle was in a big pile-up and felt excruciating pain. He realized that the coin was being ground into his upper thigh. He started yelling and kicking people to get out of the pile.

A teammate came up to Carlisle to find out what the problem was. Carlisle told him he had a half-dollar embedded in his leg.

"Instead of helping me up, he said, 'What in the hell did you think you were going to do with money out here?'

"I said, 'Joe, I didn't bring it with me, I found it out here. Help me up.'

"I had to stick my hand down the front of my pants, and when I did that the coin sank lower. Finally, at about the 50-yard line in

Quarterback Duke Carlisle played nearly one-fourth of his college games at the Cotton Bowl Stadium in Fair Park. *Cotton Bowl Athletic Association*

front of 75,000 people, I had my entire right arm jammed down into the leg of my pants.

"An official standing closest to me walked over to me.

"He said, 'You got a problem, there, son?'

"I said, 'I will be OK in a minute.'

"'I sure hope so,' the official said, 'because that doesn't look real good.'"

Hard-Hitting Horns

Before the 1964 Cotton Bowl Classic, Texas had already claimed its first national championship with a perfect 10-0 record. But a 28-6 victory over No. 2 Navy and quarterback Roger Staubach, the Heisman Trophy winner, validated the title.

"I have never been knocked down like that before," Staubach said after the game. "Yes, Texas hit harder than anyone else, much harder than Pitt. I know one thing. I will never get knocked down like that again…. Texas didn't mess around. They hit hard and they kept the pressure on all the time. No. 1, they deserve to be."

Staubach had minus-47 yards rushing. His 21 pass completions were a Navy record at the time. And his 31 attempts were his personal record at the time.

"After a game, I had never been so sore. I ran for more yardage than in any other college game I ever played in and in any professional game I have ever played in," Staubach recounted years later. "But it was all behind the line of scrimmage."

The "Staubach Drill"

Staubach's worst nightmare was Outland Trophy winner Scott Appleton. The UT strategy was to funnel "Roger the Dodger" into the clutches of the six-foot-three, 219-pound Appleton.

Appleton made 12 tackles and sacked Staubach twice for 13 yards in losses, leaving the game with eight minutes to play to a thunderous ovation when he snuffed a Navy scoring threat on fourth down at the Texas 16.

Texas held Navy without a rushing first down. Navy had minus-14 yards rushing.

"Going into that game, we had what we called the 'Staubach Drill,'" said center David McWilliams, who also played on defense. "With the ends, our whole drill after practice was to contain Staubach…. We felt like if we could keep him in the pocket, we could push him to Appleton."

The strategy worked. Appleton was named the Defensive Player of the Game.

"Appleton came up after the game and said, 'George [Brucks] and David, you are the ones who should get this trophy, because you are the ones who turned him back in,'" McWilliams said. "The whole game plan on defense was to keep him contained. We weren't really trying to hit him, because he could feel a guy on his shoulder."

Motivating Texas

UT players were incensed and motivated when Pittsburgh journalist Myron Cope wrote of UT quarterback Duke Carlisle

In 1963, Scott Appleton claimed UT's first Outland Trophy, which is given to college football's top interior lineman.
Cotton Bowl Athletic Association

before the 1964 Cotton Bowl Classic: "The Texas quarterback is a skinny-legged little kid who passes the football like a carpenter passes a wooden plank."

"We didn't just kill anybody in 1963 if you look at the scores," David McWilliams said. "We beat Oklahoma 28-7, but had to hold off Arkansas 17-13 and Rice 10-6. We had a great defense and hadn't shown much on offense. The papers said there was no way we could keep up with Staubach."

Carlisle saw the stories as well. They were pinned up on the bulletin board in the Longhorns' dressing room.

"We obviously had motivation and wanted to continue the year undefeated," Carlisle said. "In those days they declared the national champion before the bowl game. We were No. 1 and would have been terribly disappointed if we had not won. We wanted to prove [Cope] wrong."

Carlisle was named the Outstanding Back when he passed seven times for 213 yards and fired two scoring passes to Phil Harris.

"I grew up down the road in Athens [Texas], and this is where I first saw college football," Carlisle said. "I saw Doak Walker play there, and I saw Coach Bryant there when he was coaching Kentucky [the 1952 Cotton Bowl Classic]. It was my dream to play there some day. Although I went to the University of Texas, I played one-fourth of my college games at the Cotton Bowl."

Carlisle played eight of his 33 college games in the Cotton Bowl and compiled a 7-1 record there. He was 2-1 in three Cotton Bowl games, 3-0 versus OU and 2-0 versus SMU in Dallas.

Navy Coach Irks Royal

Navy coach Wayne Hardin, in a nationally televised pregame introduction at midfield, proclaimed for all the country to hear:

"When the challenger [Navy] meets the champion [Texas], and the challenger wins, then there is a new champion."

And Texas coach Darrell Royal's now famous response?

"We're ready."

"I will never forget the rush…. The best pep talk Coach Royal ever gave, 'We're ready,'" said David McWilliams.

From the Navy side, it was just pregame confidence. The Midshipmen had lost just one game all season to SMU in the very same Cotton Bowl stadium.

"We were on a roll," Navy quarterback Roger Staubach said.

"We were the No. 2 team in the country and there was just one unbeaten team in the country, the University of Texas. They felt like they deserved to be No. 1. And we very much felt like we deserved to be No. 1. We came to Dallas to prove that we were No. 1, and we proved that Texas was No. 1."

Heavy Heart

David McWilliams's mother died of a stroke four days before the game, at the age of 46.

"I finally joined the team the day before the game," McWilliams said. "Of course, I had been through all the practices. My mother loved football. I felt like she would have been disappointed if I hadn't played in the game. So I did. It was a pretty emotional game for me."

Staubach and the Navy team had sent flowers and a letter of condolences to McWilliams.

"I thought that was class," McWilliams said.

Unveiling the Wishbone

The 1969 Cotton Bowl Classic was a showcase for Texas's new Wishbone offense, which had been developed early in the season and had baffled most of the college football world. Tennessee, in a 36-13 loss to the Longhorns, was no different than eight other opponents since the offense had taken hold after an 0-1-1 Texas start.

Texas, finishing 9-1-1, with nine straight victories, rolled up 279 yards rushing and 234 passing. Quarterback James Street was dazzling. Cotton Speyrer had five catches for 161 yards, including most of the yards on two touchdown catches. Said Tennessee coach Doug Dickey: "Those two bombs really killed us."

UT's Wishbone runners overwhelmed Tennessee.

"I couldn't find a hole that wasn't open today," said UT running back Steve Worster after the game. "I had holes to run through that were so big, I couldn't believe it. That's the one thing about this team. If one hole is closed, they'll open up another for you."

Billy Dale scored this winning touchdown as Texas beat Notre Dame 21-17 in the 1970 Cotton Bowl. *Cotton Bowl Athletic Association*

A 45-Year Irish Moratorium Ends

On Saturday morning, November 22, 1969, Notre Dame ended its 45-year bowl moratorium. Cotton Bowl team selection chairman Field Scovell and the bowl's executive director Wilbur Evans, drove nearly all night to South Bend when they heard rumors Notre Dame might be eligible for a bowl for the first time since the 1925 Rose Bowl.

Scovell and Evans secured Notre Dame in a bowl coup. And the ninth-ranked Fighting Irish gave the national-champion Longhorns all they wanted before falling to Texas 21-17.

The game had all the trappings of Hollywood. Elmer Layden, Jim Crowley, and Don Miller, the surviving members of the Four Horsemen who played in the Rose Bowl 45 years earlier against Stanford, were in attendance. Former president Lyndon Johnson was there and rooted for the Longhorns, but visited both locker rooms and said it was a "fine, fine game."

UT quarterback James Street never lost a game as UT's starting quarterback, going 20-0. With Texas trailing 17-14, Street engineered a last-ditch drive against Notre Dame that went 76 yards in 17 plays. On a third-and-goal play with 1:08 left in the game, Billy Dale scored from the one-yard line as Texas finished 11-0 in the 100th season of college football.

The Historic Pass

On fourth and two from the Irish 10 with 2:26 remaining in the game, UT quarterback James Street went to the sideline to talk it over with coach Darrell Royal.

"On that fourth-down play, I thought this may be my whole football career ... just coming down to this one play," Street said. "We called Left 89 Out and Speyrer had said before that he thought he could beat his defensive man.

"I thought when I threw that the ball would get to him. I just hoped the defensive man wouldn't knock it down. If I had drilled the ball it might have been a touchdown. But me being the great passer that I am, the ball just barely got to him."

Fred Akers, a Texas assistant coach at the time, observed, "It looked like Speyrer dove eight yards. He really had to lay out to catch it. Street put it where the only person who could catch it was Speyrer. It was low and outside. And Speyrer had to stretch to get that thing. He did what was necessary to get it done."

Speyrer's Dream

The ball was thrown behind him, but Speyrer stopped, turned around, and lunged to catch the ball while on his knees.

"When I was a little guy growing up in Texas, I had many dreams about the future," Speyrer said. "And one of them involved [Cotton Bowl]. As young as five or six years old, I would sit in front of the television on New Year's Day and watch football. And, of course, I focused on the Cotton Bowl. I would sit. And I would watch. And I would dream. I would dream of one day being on that Cotton Bowl field as a player and playing, well, for the winning team.

"As I grew older, taller and skinnier, I looked more like I would be in the band than on the football team. But I would still sit in front of the TV on New Year's Day and watch the Cotton Bowl. And that dream grew...

"Walking down the tunnel versus Notre Dame, I thought this is it. This skinny kid from Port Arthur has made it. I was eager and I felt ready. Dreams do come true."

Winning Touchdown

A couple of plays later, UT's reserve halfback Billy Dale scored from the one with 1:08 remaining.

"That had to be the biggest score ever," Dale said. "And truthfully I was scared. It was an off-tackle fake to Steve Worster, the same play I ran on the drive we didn't get, when I was knocked back and came flying back three or four yards. I was worried, but I had one thought in mind—to keep my hands on the ball. Jim Bertelsen got the big block and it was a wide, wide hole."

It was the 500th victory in Texas football history. Afterward former President Lyndon Johnson went to the UT locker room and visited with Longhorns safety Freddie Steinmark, whose left leg was amputated the week after the Arkansas game. LBJ invited Steinmark and his family to the ranch.

President Richard Nixon telephoned coach Darrell Royal after the game and congratulated him on the Longhorns' victory. It further substantiated Nixon's claim a month earlier after Texas's 15-14 victory over Arkansas that UT was indeed No. 1.

"Well, Mr. President," Royal said by phone, "I am glad we did not embarrass your selection."

"You would not have embarrassed me even in defeat, for this was truly a great performance by both teams," President Nixon told Royal over the phone.

Texas's Small Lineman Matches up vs. McCoy

Texas's offensive guard, Mike Dean, all six feet and 205 pounds of him, played in three Cotton Bowls (1969-1971). But his most memorable one was in 1970 when he was blocking Notre Dame's

Mike McCoy, who was six foot five and 274 pounds and wound up later being the second overall pick in the NFL draft.

"Notre Dame came out of bowl retirement to play Texas," Dean said. "How lucky was I to be playing against the biggest defensive line in the NCAA at the time? I wouldn't be here today [Cotton Bowl Hall of Fame induction] if I had not lined up against Mike McCoy.

"No other stadium I have ever been to, the two teams are coming out of the tunnel at the same time. It reminded me of two gladiators looking at each other. You see the guy you have studied all week. You see what he looked like without his helmet on. It was an eerie feeling. The moment you stepped out of the darkness, all hell broke loose. It is the only stadium like that."

Dean noted that in the game, each team had 25 first downs and there were only three five-yard penalties and one turnover.

"The final score was 21-17," Dean said of UT's victory. "I don't think you will ever find a better game you would want to see."

A Year Later, Different Story

In the 1971 Cotton Bowl Classic, Notre Dame got its revenge, winning 24-11 and ending top-ranked Texas's 30-game winning streak.

UT quarterback Eddie Phillips accounted for 363 yards of total offense and broke Notre Dame quarterback Joe Theisman's record in the previous season's game. But on 19 occasions, Notre Dame's defense stopped Texas with no more than a yard gain or less.

"Texas had fantastic backs, just fantastic," Notre Dame defensive tackle Greg Marx said. "But this game was keyed on the tackles. We knew that if we could control Steve Worster up the middle, we could win. If we couldn't contain him, they'd control the game."

"They were large enough physically inside that we couldn't get a crease for Worster," Royal said of his star fullback. "They are a big, tough football team. That's a lot of beef they throw at you up the middle."

Worster had only 42 yards rushing on 16 carries. Phillips ran 63 yards on the first play from scrimmage. He had 164 yards on 23 carries and completed nine of 17 passes for 199 yards.

"They took away Worster and the pitch and basically left me open," Phillips said. "They covered me from the safety position. I took the gift. We lost that game because we put it on the rug [nine fumbles, five lost]. It was hard to sustain any field position."

Penn State Makes a Point in 1972 Cotton Bowl

Penn State halfback Lydell Mitchell said Nittany Lions coach Joe Paterno was unhappy that Notre Dame and Texas wound up playing for the national championship in the 1970 Cotton Bowl (for 1969 season), and the unbeaten Nittany Lions were left out of the national title picture.

Penn State finished No. 2 behind Texas in both major wire-service polls after it beat Missouri in the Orange Bowl.

"Joe never liked that," Penn State halfback Lydell Mitchell said. "When it came time to vote whether to play in the Orange Bowl or the Cotton Bowl [after the 1971 season], he made up or minds we would play in the Cotton Bowl. That game validated that Penn State could play with any team.... It was the first time Texas had been shut out [from getting a touchdown] with the Wishbone."

In the 1972 Cotton Bowl game won by Penn State 30-6, Mitchell gained 146 yards on 27 carries and scored the game's first touchdown in the third quarter.

Second Straight Cotton Loss

Texas had another bad day in the 1972 Cotton Bowl game when No. 10 Penn State drubbed the Longhorns 30-6.

Texas led 6-3 at halftime, but was outscored 27-0 in the second half and failed to score a touchdown for the first time since a 6-3 victory over Rice in October 1964, a period of 80 games.

"Fumbles played a big part, with two in the third quarter that they turned into scores," Phillips said. "I thought we still had a chance to come back at 20-6, but it looked doubtful at 23-6."

As Phillips left the field after the game, Penn State coach Joe
Paterno told him, "It was just one of those days, Eddie. You guys
kicked the ball around a little too much. It was a pleasure playing
against people like you."

The game ended the UT careers of Phillips and halfback Jim
Bertelsen, who gained only 58 yards on 14 carries.

"It has been a great four years and I wouldn't trade them for
anything, but it seems like you remember the last game the longest,
and we will remember this one for a long time," Bertelsen said after
the game.

Beating the Bear

The 1973 Cotton Bowl Classic pitted two legends against each
other, Texas coach Darrell Royal and Alabama coach Bear Bryant.
But a legendary performance by a Texas quarterback took center
stage in a 17-13 Texas victory.

"I was real sick," Texas quarterback Alan Lowry said. "My fever
was over 100 and I had chills. They gave me a shot early [in the
morning]."

Despite battling a fever and inflamed tonsils, Lowry scored the
winning touchdown on a 34-yard run with 4:22 left in the game to
lift Texas to the victory.

Lowry completed the UT rally from a 13-3 halftime deficit. He
scored his second touchdown of the second half when he hid the ball
on his hip and bootlegged to his left and ran up the sideline.

Television replays show Lowry stepping out of bounds at the
10, but he zoomed into the end zone with 4:22 remaining without
a call.

"We had been running the inside belly and we caught the
cornerback coming in," Lowry said. "We've only run the play twice
this year, and the other time was against Utah State when it went for
40 yards. I noticed the cornerback shooting in, and I told Coach
Akers about it. I think Don Ealey got a good block. I was worrying
about trying to stay in bounds."

Quarterback Alan Lowry was a hero in the Longhorns' 1973 Cotton Bowl victory over Alabama. *Cotton Bowl Athletic Association*

Mistake Bowl

The 1978 Cotton Bowl Classic turned into a Mistake Bowl for the No. 1-ranked Longhorns. Notre Dame ended Texas's unbeaten season with a 38-10 victory, which was aided by six UT turnovers (three fumbles and three pass interceptions).

"I don't want to minimize their effort at all," said Texas coach Fred Akers. "I thought and I still think we had the best football team. It was a day when they competed their hearts out. And we had turnovers deep in our end of the field. They got 30 points without having to go 30 yards. Obviously, they are proud and think they created those turnovers. And they did, some of them. But some of them were our missed plays."

Texas entered the game 11-0, but lost a chance at a national championship against the fifth-ranked Fighting Irish.

"There's not a day that goes by that I don't think about it," Outland Trophy winner Brad Shearer said later. "I mean, think about it. How many people are ever in that position?"

Beating the Bear II

A decade later, No. 6 Texas had to rally against Alabama and Bear Bryant once again. Trailing 10-0 early in the fourth quarter, it was up to another Texas quarterback to take charge.

This time junior Robert Brewer, a former walk-on, made the biggest play of the game in a 14-12 upset of No. 3 Alabama.

A 30-yard run by Brewer on a quarterback draw shocked Alabama, brought Texas within three points at 10-7, and turned the tide of the game.

"I had called another play," Texas coach Fred Akers said. "And when they came out in a man-to-man defense, Robert just called a timeout. Robert came over. And I told him if they come out in the same defense playing man, I want you to audible to the quarterback draw. He got up there and he saw we had what we wanted, and so he checked to the draw. He executed it just perfectly. We caught them by surprise."

UT center Mike Baab added, "I dropped back like we were going to set up the pass. The nose guard took the fake and rushed left. It was set up perfect. I was in the right position to block him out of the play."

Brewer remembers that Baab remarked to him when he brought in the play, "Oh, no.... Keep in mind I ran a 4.9 in the 40. I was no scatback."

"The only thing that almost became a problem," Akers said, "Herkie Walls, who could fly, I mean fly—he was one of the world's fastest young athletes at the time. He had taken his man deep, and he turned and looked back in and saw that Brewer was running up the middle, and he started going over there to congratulate him. He almost brought his defender close enough to make the tackle."

After Brewer's touchdown, Alabama made only two first downs. And sophomore fullback Terry Orr scored the winning touchdown from eight yards out with 2:05 remaining in the game.

Texans Remembering the Bear

UT quarterback Robert Brewer remembers seeing Bear Bryant at the Big Play Luncheon the day before the 1982 Cotton Bowl Classic.

"I was at a table right next to him," Brewer said. "I remember looking at these creases in his neck. There was so much character."

UT coach Fred Akers knew Bryant while he was an assistant coach.

"I had known Bear for some time," Akers said. "He was one of my mentors. He was very helpful to me when he didn't have any reason to be. He was just that way. And I thought a lot of him. You knew he might not coach another bowl game at that point in his career. You have mixed emotions. But if you get a chance to win, you win."

After the loss to Texas in the 1982 Cotton Bowl Classic, Bear Bryant finished with a 1-7-1 record against Texas.

Lost Chance

In the 1984 Cotton Bowl Classic, No. 2 Texas failed to take advantage of top-ranked Nebraska's 31-30 upset loss later in the day to Miami (Florida) in the Orange Bowl. Texas entered the game with an 11-0 record and could have claimed the national championship with a victory over Georgia.

Instead, the No. 7-ranked Bulldogs pulled out a pulsating 10-9 victory over the Longhorns.

The game swung on a fumbled punt by Craig Curry, who fumbled at the Texas 23 with 4:32 remaining. Georgia, trailing 9-3, recovered and three plays later scored the deciding touchdown and extra point.

"I tried to tell Craig, and I meant it, 'You've got to get over this,'" Texas coach Fred Akers said. "That was just one of the plays that kept us from winning the ballgame. We had so many opportunities to score and didn't, including missed field goals by a great field goal kicker, Jeff Ward. We had people open and missed them."

Confusing Situation

Texas coaches weren't sure Georgia was actually going to punt when Craig Curry fumbled, because time was running out and the Bulldogs were staring at a six-point deficit. Fearful of a fake, UT didn't put its regular punt return unit into the game.

"Michael Phelps [on the regular punt unit along with Jitter Fields] could catch it if they dropped it out of a helicopter," UT's kicker Jeff Ward said. "But it was not like we had bad people on the field. Curry was capable. It was not a personnel meltdown like people think. It was not what we wanted. It was a slight screw-up. But he knew what he was doing. The mistake was he dropped it."

In the spring of 1984, Curry was selected in the fourth round of the NFL draft by the Indianapolis Colts. He played for the Tampa Bay Buccaneers from 1984 to 1987 and the Atlanta Falcons in 1988.

Wild Day in Fair Park

In the 1991 Cotton Bowl Classic, Texas entered as the No. 3 team in the country, and Miami was No. 4. The outcome—a 46-3 Miami victory—was as shocking as the way the Hurricanes behaved before and during the game.

Miami set major bowl records at the time for penalties (16) and yards penalized (202). Before the game at the midfield coin toss, the Hurricanes lined up and stared down the Longhorns, who obviously were intimidated and committed five turnovers in the most lopsided game in Cotton Bowl history.

Miami wide receiver Randall Hill ran up the tunnel after catching a 48-yard touchdown pass in the third quarter. He was yelling, "It's too easy. It's too easy."

Another Miami wide receiver, Wesley Carroll, pranced up and down the sideline like a drum major after one of his two touchdown catches.

"They were really good and had a lot of seniors and had been together awhile," said Texas quarterback Peter Gardere, who threw three interceptions and passed for only 40 yards. "And they were fast. I remember we just weren't prepared for that. They practiced at Texas Stadium and we were supposed to practice at SMU, but the field was iced over. So we practiced at our hotel in one of the ballrooms."

"Agitated Hurricanes"

Miami defensive tackle Russell Maryland, the 1990 Outland Trophy winner, explained why the Hurricanes were upset.

"I have been apologizing for the last 10 years for that game," said Maryland, who later played for the Dallas Cowboys. "It was my last collegiate game. It was cold that week. I think it may have even snowed a little bit. We were practicing in the snow at Texas Stadium. And guys were a little bit agitated and a little bit grumpy. It was like, man, we love to be here and play in this game, but we don't want to play in this cold weather, because down in Miami we have tropic weather, so on and so forth. We were a little bit agitated.

"Then in the papers during that week one of the guys from the Longhorns started spouting off at the mouth and talking about how he was going to take my Outland Trophy away from me. It just got us a little bit mad. We got a lot of penalties that game. But the rest is history. I won't even talk about the score."

Maryland was named the outstanding defensive player of the game.

Cotton Bowling

Ricky Williams rushed for 203 yards on 30 carries in a 38-11 victory over Mississippi State in the 1999 Cotton Bowl Classic. He temporarily knocked out two Mississippi State defensive backs in the second half when he bowled over them. Tim Nelson and Kendall Roberson were laid out on the field.

"I don't think he understood what he did to them," said former UT running backs coach Bucky Godbolt, who was standing on the sideline. "I told him, 'You really hurt them. You have buried people before. But these were not little guys. These were stout guys.' The back of their heads were hitting the ground. Thank goodness it was grass and not artificial turf."

Williams's rushing total was the third best in Cotton Bowl history behind Rice's Dicky Maegle (265 yards in 1954) and Tennessee's Chuck Webb (250 yards in 1990).

Arkansas-Texas Starts the New Century

The 2000 Cotton Bowl game between Texas and Arkansas was billed as the first game of the new millennium. The Cotton Bowl staff was so concerned about security and the Y2K phenomenon that it had publicity director Charlie Fiss lead a contingent of overnighters staying in the press box to make sure everything was OK.

The UT-Arkansas game was slated for the 10 a.m. kickoff the next day. So longtime Cotton Bowl volunteers Darlene and Peter Irwin, Fred Gruhn of Kansas City, and Texas A&M-Commerce's sports information director Bill Powers all slept on the floor of the press box with the stadium lights on all night. Fiss oversaw the sleepover and kept people entertained with his witty jokes.

"We greeted the catering crew when they came in at two or three in the morning," Fiss said.

And yes, the clocks and computers worked. Texas's offense didn't, however, in a 27-6 loss, which was Texas's third straight to a major rival after falling to Texas A&M and Nebraska that season.

"Take Back Dallas"

Coach Mack Brown gave that slogan to his players before the 2003 Cotton Bowl Classic against LSU. The Longhorns had lost five straight games in Dallas: the 2000 Cotton Bowl Classic against Arkansas (27-6), three straight Texas-OU games, and the 2001 Big 12 Championship game against Colorado (39-37). They took back Dallas in a big way with a 35-20 victory over LSU.

"There is no way you can win the Big 12 without coming through Dallas," said Texas cornerback Rod Babers the week before the game. "So they need to know we can win in Dallas."

CHAPTER EIGHT

Big Earl Rambles, Royal Exits

Earl Campbell played at Texas from 1974 to 1977 and became the school's first Heisman Trophy winner when he claimed the award his senior season. Over the course of his career at Texas, Campbell, nicknamed "The Tyler Rose," rushed for 4,443 yards and 40 touchdowns.

Campbell was recruited by coach Darrell Royal and played for the Texas legend three years before starring in his final collegiate season for coach Fred Akers in 1977. Campbell was selected No. 1 in the NFL draft by the Houston Oilers and went on to a stellar pro career in which he rushed for 9,407 yards and 74 touchdowns and was a five-time All-Pro selection.

Campbell's Recruitment

Ann Campbell raised 11 children—seven boys and four girls—on a 100-acre farm five miles east of Tyler, Texas. Earl's father died when he was 10 in 1966.

"The best coach he has ever had was his mom," said Texas coach Fred Akers.

Campbell, who was the fifth oldest child in the Campbell family, played mostly linebacker for the John Tyler High School Roses his junior season. He believed his future was at linebacker. But Campbell had to play running back his senior year because his coach, Corky Nelson, came by his house during the summer and told Earl he didn't have any running backs.

"I always wanted to be a linebacker," Earl said. "I was bow-legged and built like Mike Ditka. He was my hero. I used to run to the line of scrimmage and throw the ball down on purpose. Corky said, 'I will let you be a middle linebacker and a running back.'"

As Campbell started running the ball, UT coach Darrell Royal began to take notice.

Texas wasn't the only school paying attention, though. Baylor and Houston also recruited Campbell, who limited his options to those three schools. He said a prayer one night, woke up, and committed to Texas.

Dispelling a Myth

Campbell said that when UT coach Darrell Royal began recruiting him he listened to the gossip at the local barbershop in Tyler where he had been going since the sixth grade.

"They said what a racist this guy was," Campbell said. "When I got a chance to go to the university, I made a point of becoming a friend. If he didn't want to be a friend, then all the things they said about him were true. I learned a lot from him like how to handle the media and people. He was a lot like my father. I had lost my father in fifth grade… Coach Royal and I have a great relationship. So do I and Coach Akers."

"Earl wasn't a secret," Royal said. "Everybody wanted Earl. He was the No. 1 recruit. With his size, speed, and ability, he dominated high school football."

Earl on Special Teams

In a 38-7 victory over Arkansas in 1974, freshman fullback Earl Campbell blocked a Razorbacks punt right before the half and

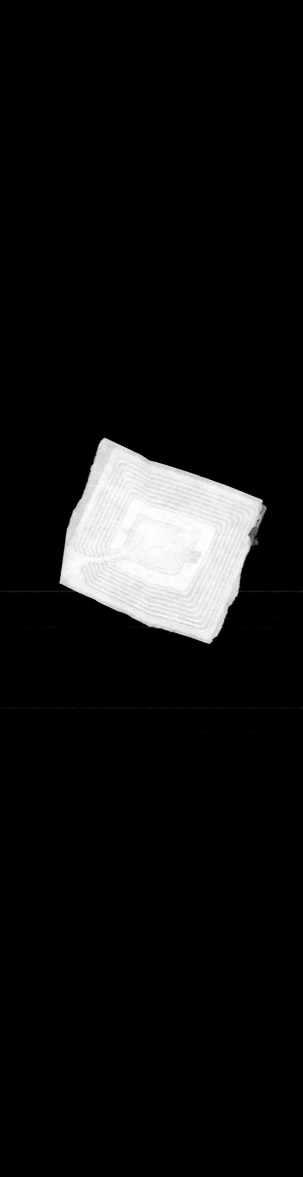

defensive tackle Doug English carried it into the end zone. It was English's only touchdown at Texas.

"The main thing he did was, you know a lot of people go in there and sort of flinch off to the side or something," said UT coach Darrell Royal after the game. "He just went right smack into it."

"He was a real quick running back, and the coaches inserted him at nose tackle because they figured the upback wouldn't be able to cross over fast enough to block him," English told *Horns Illustrated*. "So he went right through and blocked the punt."

English, who started every UT game from 1972 to 1974, later was a four-time All-Pro defensive lineman for the Detroit Lions between 1975 and 1985. But even he was impressed with the young freshman.

Back of Few Words

Earl Campbell was just a freshman in 1974 and he kept to himself.

He didn't open up much even to his teammates until after Texas beat No. 8 Texas A&M 32-3.

"I will never forget what happened right after the Texas A&M game," said UT offensive tackle Bob Simmons. "Coach Royal had made this little talk, and Earl asked if he could say something. He got up on a bench and asked for silence. I thought, 'Here comes a rah-rah, gung-ho speech.' He suddenly struck a silly pose and yelled, 'Ain't I cute?' It broke everybody up."

Campbell rushed for 928 yards and six touchdowns as a freshman fullback and was named All-Southwest Conference.

"When he was a freshman, I coached Earl," Akers said. "I was a young running backs coach…. He made me a helluva coach."

Springtime with Earl

Spring practice during the Earl Campbell years was a tough time for the UT defensive players.

"I just remember in spring training you hated to scrimmage him," said David McWilliams, who was a UT assistant defensive coach when Campbell was a player. "You weren't worried about him getting hurt as much as him hurting somebody. He was such a bull."

One day UT defensive coordinator Mike Campbell came up with a new defensive coverage.

"We were going to take away everything inside on run yardage and not let them get outside and give it to the fullback, and the safety was going to come up and tackle the fullback," McWilliams recalled. "Well, they handed it to Earl at fullback and we had a little safety about 155 pounds and Earl knocked him out.

"And I remember Mike Campbell said, 'What was that?'

"I said, 'You told me to call that, Coach.'

"'Well, don't call that anymore even if I tell you to. We aren't going to have a safety left.'"

Sophomore Superlatives

Campbell, still playing fullback as a sophomore, went over the 1,000-yard mark rushing with 1,118 yards and scored 13 touchdowns. Texas went 9-2 during the regular season and tied for first in the Southwest Conference with Texas A&M and Arkansas.

"From the standpoint of running the ball and breakaway speed, I don't think there was [an equal]," David McWilliams said. "People said he didn't catch the ball. Well, we didn't throw it. So what?"

Campbell only caught six passes for 128 yards and one touchdown during his four seasons at UT.

Moving to Tailback

Campbell was moved to tailback his junior season in 1976. But a hamstring injury forced him to miss four games during Darrell Royal's final season as head coach.

Royal had lasting memories of Campbell, who, at every level, was challenged by skeptics. Royal said at each level Campbell excelled. Before Campbell played at Texas, skeptics said he could run over high school players, but wouldn't do it in college. And then in the pros...

Earl Campbell, "The Tyler Rose," is one of two UT Heisman Trophy winners. *Cotton Bowl Athletic Association*

"They said he was going to be playing with the big boys there and he wouldn't run over them," Royal quipped. "Well, he ran over them, too."

Earl Says Bye to Darrell

In 1976, Texas defeated Arkansas 29-12 in Royal's last game at Texas during a disappointing 5-5-1 season.

Royal talked to reporters at the back of the dressing room. Campbell climbed atop a chair and waved at Royal. Royal smiled and waved back.

"Thanks for coming by, Earl," Royal said.

It was also the final game for Arkansas coach Frank Broyles, whose record fell to 5-14 against UT and Royal.

Following Darrell

After the 1976 season, Royal wanted longtime assistant coach and defensive coordinator Mike Campbell, 54, to become his successor. Royal stepped aside to become the school's athletic director.

But a seven-person committee, which was headed by UT president Lorene Rogers, chose former UT assistant Fred Akers, 38, as the new head coach. Akers had been head coach at Wyoming for two seasons.

It was a shocking choice to some, particularly when a headline ran in the *Austin American-Statesman* on December 15, "'It's Mike— Mike Campbell was named the University of Texas's 25th head football coach today, replacing Darrell Royal, who resigned December 4."

The next day: "It wasn't Mike.... We goofed.... Our faces are red."

Why were Royal's wishes not granted? Columnists and writers across the state surmised that Rogers wanted to show Royal who was the boss at UT.

Campbell, who seven years earlier had turned down a chance to become the Baylor head coach, was not rewarded for his loyalty. He left coaching and did not join Akers's staff.

A Receiver Is Born

In a 1977 season-opening 44-0 victory over Boston College, Campbell caught the first pass reception of his career in the first game of the new Fred Akers era. He had caught a two-point conversion pass in the 1975 Bluebonnet victory over Colorado.

"I want to catch passes," said Campbell, who weighed 220 pounds going into his senior season. "I have watched Chuck Foreman on TV, and I don't think it is any secret that I want to play professional football. Foreman combines the pass, catching and running. I would like to. And I think I can, too."

Akers utilized Campbell as a halfback in the Veer and I-back in the I, but liked to have the option of using Campbell as a wide receiver.

"You wouldn't want to make a training film out of his style," Akers said. "But he has not dropped a single pass we've thrown him in practice, nor did he drop one [versus Boston College]."

The most important catch of his career occurred four games later against Arkansas. It was a 28-yarder that helped set up a touchdown in a 13-9 UT victory.

Famous Photo

One of the most famous pictures of Earl Campbell was taken during his Heisman Trophy-winning season of 1977 at the Cotton Bowl stadium in a game against SMU. Texas won the game 30-14 as Campbell rushed for 213 yards on 32 carries.

The picture, which has been widely distributed among UT alums, shows Campbell bowling over an SMU player who is lying on the field.

"I remember it well," said former SMU linebacker Putt Choate. "It is No. 36 Sid Greehey, one of our safeties at the time. Sid slipped as Earl cut, and it made it look like Earl ran over him. I don't think they even made contact, but the camera angle made it look that way. Sid was mad about the photo then. We kidded him relentlessly about it being in the paper."

Bowling 'Em over

During a 35-21 victory at Houston in 1977, Campbell ran into a photographer, who slammed into Texas's mascot Bevo in the end zone. Campbell gained 173 yards and scored three touchdowns despite suffering from a virus.

Former Texas coach Darrell Royal said, "I know 12 people who won't have any trouble sleeping tonight—Earl and the 11 guys who were trying to tackle him."

130 TALES FROM THE TEXAS LONGHORNS

"A long time ago someone said to me, 'A person is not measured by the breaths he takes, but by the breathless moments he creates,'" Fred Akers said. "And he has created more breathless moments than anybody I have ever been around."

Fitting End

Aggies defensive end Phil Bennett, later an SMU head coach, said after UT crushed A&M 57-28, "If he doesn't win the Heisman Trophy, they ought to throw it away."

Campbell, coming out of the backfield, caught a 60-yard pass uncontested from quarterback Randy McEachern. It was the only touchdown reception of Campbell's collegiate career.

Texas A&M linebacker coach John Paul Young said, "They ran a play we hadn't seen them run before, a bootleg throwback pass. It was a tremendous pass and a tremendous call."

Campbell had a career-high 222 yards against the Aggies in his last regular-season game. It was the third and final 200-yard rushing game of his career.

March to the Heisman

In 1977, Earl Campbell was the NCAA rushing and scoring champion his senior year with 1,744 yards (158.5 yards a game) and 19 touchdowns (18 rushing). The only game in which he failed to rush for 100 yards was the season opener against Boston College, an easy 44-0 victory.

But he never had fewer than 116 yards after the opener and twice went over the 200-yard mark during the 1977 season.

"The thing about Earl, we didn't play him the whole game except maybe three games his senior year," Akers said. "He gained all those yards hardly playing in the second half. We didn't think there was any point of him being out on the field, if we had it won. There's no telling how many yards he would have racked up."

Humorous Earl

When Tony Dorsett won the Heisman Trophy in 1976, he corrected the presenter's pronunciation of his last name when he didn't put the emphasis on the SETT.

"It is Dor-SETT," he said.

When Earl Campbell was awarded the Heisman Trophy a year later, he quipped, "It is Cam-BELL!"

Campbell-Doak Walker Connection

Despite the fact that they played three decades apart, Earl Campbell had a strong relationship with another Heisman Trophy winner, SMU's Doak Walker (1948). When the late Walker started his banquet in 1990 for current players, it wasn't what it is today.

"I got to be very good friends with Doak and Skeeter [Walker's second wife]," Campbell said. "I remember coming to this banquet … and it was five tables, then 10 tables, then 25 tables. It just kept getting bigger and bigger."

In 1998, a Doak Walker Legends Award was added.

"I told [Doak], I helped you get this started and you selected Gale Sayers and then another person got it,'" Campbell said in jest. "'What about me?'"

Although Walker had passed away, Campbell became the fifth recipient in January 2003.

"This is like being the President of the United States and then later having a chance to win the Nobel Peace Prize," Campbell said. "There is nothing else you can do."

Former UT coach Fred Akers presented Campbell with his Legends Award.

"The two of them [Campbell and Walker] were very much alike," Akers said. "They were electric. Any time they got the ball people in the stadium would stand up because something was going to happen. There were about seven different explosions every time he carried the ball."

Campbell's Small Spinal Cord

Earl Campbell said in January 2003, that he could have been paralyzed during his playing days because he had a small spinal cord.

"I found out I had a very small spinal cord," Campbell said. "Because all my muscles were so big, it never popped, but it might have and I could have been paralyzed. But I never got off the field fast. I got up slow."

CHAPTER NINE

The Akers Years

Fred Akers, a former UT assistant, succeeded the legendary Darrell Royal as head coach starting with the 1977 season. During his tenure, Akers won two Southwest Conference championships, took the Longhorns to nine bowls in 10 seasons, and finished in the top 10 four times.

Akers, who left Wyoming for Austin after only two seasons, said he believed longtime UT assistant coach Mike Campbell would be offered the UT head job upon Royal's retirement.

"But I wasn't sure he wanted it, because Mike was a pure football guy," Akers said. "We had discussions before when I was an assistant. He said, 'I just want to coach.' I thought Mike would be the next coach, but when you saw it was not going to be that way, I was thrilled to be offered the job."

Akers told Wyoming officials when he took the job that there were only two schools he would leave Laramie for: his alma mater Arkansas or Texas. Each job opened up at the same time with Royal and Frank Broyles retiring after the 1976 season. And Texas got to Akers first.

A Stellar Beginning

Akers's first Texas team went 11-0 out of the gate. Midway through the 1977 season, the Longhorns rose to the No. 1 ranking

Coach Fred Akers came within a 10-9 loss to Georgia in the 1984
Cotton Bowl of compiling a perfect season. *Cotton Bowl Athletic Association*

after a 30-14 victory over SMU. And they held that throughout the
rest of the regular season before meeting Notre Dame in the 1978
Cotton Bowl Classic.

"We had a very good defense, and in the early games your
defense always sets the tone," Akers said. "We had a balanced
football team, throwing for as many yards as we were running,
which was a different look for Texas. We had a great running back

in Earl Campbell, who could dominate a game. It wasn't just him. We had a couple of wide receivers who really made it tough on defenses concentrating on getting too close to the line of scrimmage, Alfred Jackson and Johnny 'Lam' Jones. Both of them were threats and had good long careers in the NFL."

Earl the Receiver

One of the most difficult two-game stretches for any coach was playing two big rivals back to back. Fred Akers faced that during his inaugural UT season in 1977 when Texas beat No. 2 Oklahoma 13-6, and then had to travel to No. 8 Arkansas the following week.

Texas won the Arkansas game 13-9 and didn't have another close game during the regular season. Texas was trailing when Akers decided to fake a reverse to Lam Jones, who was a threat as a runner. UT then threw the ball to big Earl Campbell.

"We faked a reverse to him and were able to sneak Earl Campbell out in the flat in the opposite direction," Akers said of the 28-yard pass reception. "And he went down to the one-yard line. And Lam Jones knocked it in for the touchdown. It was such a good play and a sudden play. It was a shut-the-crowd-up or quiet-them-down kind of football play. They were shocked. They were sure Lam Jones had the ball."

Going to Arkansas

Akers, the former Razorbacks player, compiled a 7-3 coaching record against his alma mater.

"My pastor tells a story which pretty well sums up the first time I went in there [as Texas head coach]," Akers said of UT's 13-9 victory in 1977.

"He said you know I had an offer to do a revival in Arkansas. He said I kind of remembered how it was during that Big Shootout up there [in 1969]. I was concerned. I asked the Lord, 'Would You go with me when I go up there to Arkansas?' And He answered my prayer. He said, 'I will go with you as far as Texarkana.'"

It wound up being Earl Campbell and field goal kickers who were the stars of the game. UT's Russell Erxleben (1975-1978) kicked field goals of 58 and 52 yards in the first quarter. Arkansas's Steve Little kicked three, including a 67-yarder, which tied Erxleben's NCAA record (with a tee).

"He was not just a great kicker; he was a great punter," Akers said of Erxleben. "He could hit 67-yard field goals or 67-yard punts. When you have a guy like that, everybody knows about him."

"Lam" Jones, the Athlete

Johnny "Lam" Jones (1976-1979), who was raised by his grandparents from the ninth grade on, was timed at 4.34 seconds in the 40-yard dash. He was the second pick of the entire draft by New York Jets in 1980.

"There is no wide receiver in the country with his talent," Akers said. "There are some with more experience as a receiver, but none with his abilities. Johnny is so tough, too. That's something the average person doesn't see. He is such a beautiful athlete. He just sort of glides along."

Jones worked with six different quarterbacks during his four years at UT, but led the team in receiving three of those years. After his senior season in high school, he won a gold medal as part of the U.S. 400-meter relay team at the 1976 Olympics and finished sixth in the 100-meter dash.

He was nicknamed Lam Jones to distinguish himself from A. J. "Ham" Jones, who played for UT from 1978 to 1981. Lam is from Lampasas, Texas; Ham is from Hamlin, Texas.

"[Lam Jones] was not just a track man," Akers said. "He was fast and could play football. He was a football man who could fly on the track. He was a threat as a runner. And he was aggressive. He could have been a running back and played there as a freshman [when he had 182 yards rushing against Rice]. He was not a fragile guy. He had more than just speed. He was something to see."

Another Outland Trophy Winner

Brad Shearer, a six-foot-four, 255-pound senior tackle, anchored a defense that did not allow a touchdown until the sixth game of the 1977 season against SMU. He became UT's third

Brad Shearer, shown here tackling Texas A&M quarterback David Walker, anchored a UT defense that did not allow a touchdown until the sixth game of the 1977 season. *Cotton Bowl Athletic Association*

Outland Trophy winner, following Scott Appleton (1963) and Tommy Nobis (1965).

"Shearer didn't win that trophy by accident," Fred Akers said. "Brad was an outstanding defensive tackle. He enjoyed everything. He had a good sense of humor. He didn't take himself too seriously. He would compete, especially against the run. You would play teams that would run the ball. He was awfully tough on those offensive linemen."

Shearer, from Austin, was also recruited by Oklahoma.

"When I went up to visit, the OU coaches told me the Texas coaches were so old that they would die before I graduated," Shearer once said. "I never even thought about going there. As a matter of fact, I tried to talk some of the recruits into going to Texas."

By the ninth game of 1974 (Shearer's freshman season), injuries opened up a starting spot at defensive tackle. He started every game the rest of his career there. He starred as a sophomore in 1975, battled injuries as a junior, and won the Outland Trophy as a senior.

In the 1975 Arkansas game, Shearer had a pass interception that led to the game-winning touchdown for the Longhorns. In the 1975 OU game, Shearer played great against Terry Webb, Oklahoma's All-America guard, in UT's 24-17 loss to OU.

Shearer was picked in the third round of the 1978 NFL draft by the Chicago Bears.

Johnson Emerges as Star

From 1976 to 1979, UT safety Johnnie Johnson (from LaGrange High School) recorded 13 interceptions, 282 tackles, and returned punts for more than 1,000 yards.

During coach Darrell Royal's final season in 1976, Johnson moved into the starting lineup as a freshman. He was a major part of the tough defense in 1977 that did not allow a touchdown until the sixth game of the season after the Oklahoma and Arkansas games.

In 1979, Johnson was part of a defense that gave up only nine points per game (17 was the most). That defensive team produced seven draft picks in the 1980 NFL draft. That included four defensive backs: Johnson (first round, Los Angeles Rams), Derrick Hatchett (first round, Baltimore Colts), Ricky Churchman (fourth round, San Francisco 49ers), and Charles Vaclavik (12th round, Pittsburgh Steelers).

Johnson, a four-sport star in high school, was eighth of 11 children (five boys and six girls) and grew up on a ranch about five miles outside of LaGrange. He hauled 40- to 60-pound bales of hay from sunup to sundown.

"He was one of those guys who got some votes for the Heisman," Akers said. "He was just outstanding at every level. He didn't just line up and make those interceptions and tackles. He was a heck of a punt returner. This guy had courage few have. And he was very, very coachable and a good leader. He could play corner and safety. And anybody who plays corner knows that is a real chore."

Swallowing the Worm

In 1978, a 2-8 Baylor team upset No. 9 Texas 38-14. It is remembered as the "Worm Game."

Baylor coach Grant Teaff told his team a story before the game about two Eskimos who were ice fishing. Both were using identical equipment. One was successful. The other was not.

The Eskimo not catching fish asked the other why he was catching fish. The Eskimo told his buddy: "You have to keep the worms warm." He took one out of his mouth and put it on the hook. Teaff took a warm worm from his pocket and popped it in his mouth.

That was the only motivation the Bears needed.

"You can understand why I would like to forget it," Akers said. "Baylor had good football teams back then. Baylor had enough athletes to play with anybody without Grant chewing on those worms. That was something, I will tell you. Grant was a good motivator, though."

Sun Bowl: Texas Wind Knowledge

Maryland coach Jerry Claiborne was a good coach. But he didn't understand West Texas wind in a 42-0 loss to Texas in the 1978 Sun Bowl.

"Maryland got started off on the wrong foot," Akers said. "First of all, they won the toss and they elected to receive. [Texas took the wind.] And there was a 35-mile-an-hour wind out there. They never recovered."

Small Texas Town, Big Recruit

Texas's six-foot-two defensive tackle Steve McMichael (1976-1979) was from Freer, a small ranch town in south Texas. He could play several positions for the Longhorns.

"Steve never thought anybody could beat him at anything," Akers said. "He was a handful.... He was a warrior, a battler, like Brad Shearer. Steve was an All-American, but the NFL was a little reluctant because of his height. They thought if you weren't six foot four or six foot five as a defensive lineman you couldn't play in the NFL. He was drafted by the Patriots, who didn't think he could do it, so not long after they sent him to Chicago and he had a 14-year career there. He was a real battler and never thought six foot two was a handicap."

One for the Clinic

Texas played a nearly flawless defensive game at No. 5 Missouri during the second game of the 1979 season and won 21-0. It was so good that Texas used it to show future players how the game should be played.

Missouri had an explosive team led by quarterback Phil Bradley.

"That game was like a clinic for our defense," Akers said. "In fact, we used that game to teach a lot of our players.... We would take our incoming classes, freshmen, and show them that.... Bradley was good. They could run up and down the field."

A guest coach on the Texas sideline that day was Ernie Koy Sr., who had scored 24 points in UT's 65-0 victory over Missouri in 1932 on the very same field in Columbia, Missouri. Koy was recognized by the game's public address announcer.

"They stood up and gave him a standing ovation," Akers said. "I thought that was a real sportsmanlike gesture for their crowd."

Jersey Talk

During the 1979 and 1980 seasons, Texas rose to a No. 2 ranking in both seasons, but each year the team stumbled and didn't win the Southwest Conference title.

Akers was in a particularly irritable mood in 1980. The Longhorns were No. 2 before falling to SMU 20-6. That started a tailspin that saw Texas lose four of its last six regular-season games to tumble out of the ratings.

Preparing for a Bluebonnet Bowl game against North Carolina, Akers was railing on his team in a meeting. Jitter Fields, a five-foot-five freshman walk-on defensive back from Dallas, raised his hand in the midst of the tirade.

"Coach, think we can get names on the back of our uniforms next year?" Fields asked.

Akers got a smirk on face. He started to laugh. Then everybody in the room started to laugh. And the next season in 1981, the UT players had their names on the back of the uniforms for the first time.

Finding a Quarterback

The 1981 season was much better (10-1-1) thanks to a decision Akers made at quarterback during a 14-14 tie with Houston at the Astrodome. The Longhorns trailed 14-0 in the first half, with quarterback Rick McIvor getting dinged trying to make a defensive play.

"We went in at halftime and we just had a turnover," said UT's former walk-on quarterback Robert Brewer. "There was an interception on a screen pass, and [McIvor] was trying to make a tackle on that play. We all ran off the field for the locker room. I remember the coaches didn't come out to talk to us as quickly as they normally did. They were having a pow-wow."

Brewer said they were trying to decide what to do at quarterback, whether to put him or Donnie Little in at quarterback or go with woozy McIvor. Akers told Brewer the game was in his hands as they went out for the second half.

Receiver Herkie Walls looked at Brewer and said, "You are not the No. 2 quarterback no more, so don't play like it."

Brewer said he got knocked "goofy the fourth or fifth play" of the second half and for a couple of series didn't know what was going on. But he led Texas to two touchdowns to tie the score 14-14.

The tie proved significant because it meant Texas would finish in second place in the SWC by itself, ahead of Houston. And with SWC champion SMU ineligible for postseason play, UT went to the Cotton Bowl.

Brewer Was a Surprise

Robert Brewer, from Richardson, Texas, met Fred Akers several years before and told him he was going to play quarterback for him. Akers merely saw a skinny kid nobody was recruiting.

"We didn't offer him a scholarship when he was a senior and hardly anybody else did," Akers said. "He came to Texas as a walk-on. He not only won a scholarship, he was elected captain of the team."

Brewer, whose father played quarterback for UT in the early 1950s and whose uncle was an OU quarterback in the late 1940s, became UT's main quarterback after the Houston game. He was a junior when he finally got his big chance, but he remembered what Akers had told him early in his career.

"I remember going down there in the spring," Brewer said. "Coach Akers was in office, and I asked him, 'Can I have any kind of chance?' He told me, If you are good enough, you will get a chance.'"

Quarterback Leaders

Akers said UT quarterbacks weren't always the greatest passers or the fanciest runners. They often weren't the best players on the team. But they won.

"Sometimes your best leaders aren't the best players," Akers said. "They have something when they step in that huddle that makes the other 10 guys get better."

Akers said UT Wishbone quarterbacks James Street and Eddie Phillips in the late 1960s and early 1970s weren't judged fairly because of that running offense.

"That was something that made people think we didn't have good quarterbacks because we didn't throw the ball a lot," Akers said. "They were measuring their ability to throw rather than their ability to lead and to win. Texas quarterbacks have been leaders and winners. Randy McEachern, Robert Brewer, Peter Gardere, and James Brown are in the same mold, too."

Brewer to Walls

Quarterback Robert Brewer showed that leadership during the 1982 season, when he led the Longhorns to a 9-2 record. UT lost back-to-back games against Oklahoma and SMU during the regular season.

"We didn't have a quarterback that was big, strong, and fast, and we didn't have a scatback at running back," Brewer said. "Herkie Walls made our offense go. He was blinding fast. We would stretch the field with the passing game. And we ran a lot of reverses with him. We had a lot of fun."

Brewer threw a school-record (at the time) 12 touchdown passes, and Walls had 10 touchdowns on pass receptions in 1982.

But practicing on Christmas Day, Brewer suffered a broken thumb and was lost for a Sun Bowl date with North Carolina. He was replaced by freshman Todd Dodge.

"I always dreamed of a white Christmas. I never dreamed it would come on my first college start [at the Sun Bowl]," Dodge quipped. He completed just six of 22 passes for 50 yards in the 1982 Sun Bowl, which was played in the snow and won by North Carolina 26-10.

But the disappointment of losing the Sun Bowl was turned into an experience well learned for Todd Dodge, who would play quarterback for Texas through 1985 and was the starter at the beginning of the 1984 season.

Kicking with Ward

A freshman kicker named Jeff Ward became a major UT offensive weapon, starting with the 1983 season-opening win at Auburn 20-7.

He had been recruited for other positions at other schools.

"I knew I would be an average wide receiver," Ward said. "I knew I could be a good field goal kicker if that's all I did. I doubted they were thrilled that an 18-year-old could be their difference maker. But the first game on the road against Bo Jackson, I won [coach Fred Akers] over.

"He knew I was a player who was confident. If he would ask me, 'Can you make it here?' If I said, 'Yes,' he knew I could deliver the goods."

Ward's kicking was pivotal in two games during the 1983 season in a 9-3 nailbiter over Houston at the Astrodome, where people booed every time the Longhorns went onto the field. Ward's 52-yarder also was the difference in a 15-12 win over SMU.

Said Ward of the SMU game, "I don't ever remember being on the field with that much talent. We had All-Americans all over the place. We had 17 guys get drafted. Man for man they had almost as many good players as we did. We knew points would be hard to come by. And I am sure they knew the same thing."

The Edwin Simmons Story

No. 2-ranked Texas entered the game against No. 8 Oklahoma with a 4-0 record. The game served as the coming out and ending party for sic-foot-four, 230-pound sophomore running back Edwin Simmons.

He rushed for 100 yards on 14 carries in a 28-16 UT victory over the Sooners.

"Had he been healthy, it would have been Ricky Williams's numbers before Ricky Williams," said UT kicker Jeff Ward.

The very next week, early in UT's 31-3 victory at Arkansas, Simmons went out with a serious knee injury and never was the same again. He had a series of knee operations.

"Simmons was due to be really special; he was the best running back in the nation," Akers said. "Against Arkansas he got hurt the first time he carried the ball. He had fragile kneecaps. He was like one of those sprinters as opposed to someone slightly bow-legged who was used to putting pressure on kneecaps. That condition is more prevalent among women athletes."

Leiding's Bulletin Board Material

Texas's biggest game the rest of the 1983 season was at No. 9 SMU. The year before the Mustangs had defeated Texas 30-17, when Texas linebacker Jeff Leiding made some very unflattering remarks about SMU.

"They were stouter than 10 acres of onions," Akers said of the 1983 SMU team.

"The year before Jeff had just ridiculed SMU publicly. And SMU played their rear ends off against us. I brought Jeff in personally and I told him, 'Listen, we are getting ready to play this ballgame and we are not going to turn it into a rasslin' match publicity-wise.'

"It was a joke, all this going back and forth," Akers continued. "The banter before the ballgame was more important than the game. I said, 'We are not getting involved with that anymore. I am telling you now, if you can't say something good about 'em, then you don't say anything. That's it.'"

The reporters in their weekly question-and-answer session with UT players baited Leiding: "What do you think of SMU this year?"

"Coach Akers told me if I couldn't say anything good about them, not to say anything," Leiding told reporters. "I ain't saying nothing."

UT won 15-12.

"We laughed about it," Akers said "He was very playful. It wasn't life and death for him all the time."

Great Start in 1984

After a disappointing loss to Georgia in the 1984 Cotton Bowl Classic cost the Longhorns the national title, the 1984 season started well with victories over good Auburn and Penn State teams.

Akers remembers the opener against Auburn, won by the Longhorns 35-27.

"Todd Dodge, our quarterback, was a 4.5 40-yard guy," Akers said. "And you would bootleg with him. But he could barely make the corner versus Auburn's defensive ends. In fact that's the game that Jerry Gray ran down Bo Jackson. Bo broke a run and went about 60 with it. Jerry caught him and threw him out of bounds. Bo dislocated his shoulder and was out a few games in that season."

No. 2 Texas followed that showing with a 28-3 victory over fourth-ranked Penn State in East Rutherford, New Jersey.

"Penn State was probably a shocker to some people because we really dominated them," Akers said. "And that's not what you usually do against Penn State. It happened to be the first of a three-game series, and we played it at a neutral site."

Another Top Defensive Back

Jerry Gray was a consensus All-Amercan at Texas during the 1983 and 1984 seasons. He led the Longhorns with 10.5 tackles per game as a junior, and in each of his final two seasons he recovered three fumbles. As a senior, he intercepted seven passes.

"Jerry Gray was like Johnny Johnson," Akers said. He was in the same category. Jerry was like another coach out there on the field. He was just a tremendously talented player. "He played cornerback as well as safety. He wanted to know everything about it. It wasn't enough to know just what his position was or even all the secondary; he wanted to know what the linebacker's responsibility was. And that is one of the big reasons he is a defensive coordinator today in the NFL [for Buffalo]. He is one of those young guys extremely capable of being a coach in the NFL."

Texas's Dream Draft

The 1984 NFL draft produced 17 Texas draft picks—more than any other draft in history. That number rose to 18 when the supplemental draft was added. Cornerback Mossy Cade was the only first-round pick (San Diego Chargers).

There were five UT offensive linemen selected in that draft, led by tackle Doug Dawson who was taken in the second round by the St. Louis Cardinals. And there were nine defensive players selected in the same draft.

"[Dawson] was a four-year starter," Akers said. "He was a top student and a top football player. He was very sharp, smart. He was kind of like a coach being out there on the offensive line. He knew what everybody was supposed to do. He rarely made mistakes."

Ward Key in Several Games

In 1984, in a 13-10 victory over Texas Tech, Ward kicked a 25-yard field goal to tie the score 10-10. Then with three seconds left, he kicked a 35-yard field goal to win the game after his roommate and quarterback Todd Dodge directed a last-ditch drive.

In 1985, Ward set a UT record with five field goals in a 15-13 victory over Arkansas, including a 55-yarder. The field-goal mark was later tied when Kris Stockton kicked five field goals in a 29-17 victory at Texas Tech during the 2000 season.

"It sounds crazy to plan to kick a field goal," Ward said. "But we reached a point where our defense was good enough. We didn't need to take risks."

Ward and coach Fred Akers had a very good working relationship. Akers would simply ask him if he could make it.

"He knew I wanted the truth," Akers said. "He would say, 'I am good from here. Here it is a tossup.'

"I also let Jeff pretty much coach the holders. I had two kickers who I think knew a great deal about the kicking game. Raul Allegre ... was a phenomenal kicker, too. He kicked for several years in the NFL. He could kick onside kicks so many different ways. They were both [former] soccer players. Jeff knew more about holders than any player I ever coached."

Akers's Last Seasons

As cheating intensified in the Southwest Conference in the mid-1980s, Texas's talent level dipped dramatically. And so did UT's win levels. During Akers's final three seasons (1984-1986), Texas had a combined record of 20-14-1. Akers was 5-6 in 1986 and was fired.

"There was no doubt my senior year [1986], we had slipped in talent," kicker Jeff Ward said. "We didn't have as many good players as '83 or '84. Many of the players Texas [would] have gotten were getting paid off. No matter how good a recruiting pitch was, guys who normally would visit Texas weren't. We still got good players. But from the class of '84, 17 players were drafted. Guys were going other places in '86 and '87. And 5-6 was unacceptable."

Ward also said losing to Georgia in the 1984 Cotton Bowl Classic hurt Akers.

"Had we beaten Georgia that day and went on to be national champions, he would be safe for a long, long time. There was an expectation, we kept getting close, but we didn't deliver the goods."

CHAPTER TEN

Mc and Mac Eras

Tech Stop: For One Season

Longtime UT assistant and former player David McWilliams spent one season as the Texas Tech coach in 1986 when Red Raiders athletic director T. Jones came calling. The places McWilliams always thought he would like to coach were Texas, TCU, Texas Tech, and Texas A&M.

"A&M probably was never going to hire me," McWilliams said. "So it was Tech and TCU. I liked Fort Worth because I had grown up south of there. I wanted to be a head coach, and Tech would be a great place to be…. The only other place I would want to be was Texas. And in my mind, I didn't think this job was going to come open in a year. I felt Fred Akers was going to be [at Texas] another three years at least and maybe longer."

But after 10 seasons, Akers was fired following a 5-6 overall record and 4-4 (fifth place) finish in the Southwest Conference. It was the third straight season Texas had failed to win the league title.

McWilliams Lured Back to Austin

UT athletic director DeLoss Dodds offered McWilliams the job. But McWilliams still wasn't sure he wanted to take it because he had only been at Texas Tech the one season.

So he called coach Darrell Royal.

"I hated to leave after a year," McWilliams told Royal. "He said, 'I know it.' I told him they need me. He said, 'Texas needs you, too. You had 20 years here and your family and all of that. You do what you think.' I went home and talked to my wife. And I said we have to go back. Probably the hardest thing in the world was to tell T. Jones.

"People got on me. But they really got on T. The second hardest thing was to go to the team. And I will never forget, [Texas Tech quarterback] Billy Joe Tolliver said, 'I understand and the players understand and we wish you the best of luck. But we are going to beat your butt next year.' The next year we played them in Austin and we beat them (41-27), but then the next year Billy Joe beat us late in the game (33-32). He took them down for a touchdown."

Slow Start, Then...

In 1987, Texas lost three of its first five games under McWilliams, but the defining moment of the first season came in the sixth game against old rival No. 15 Arkansas.

Texas won 16-14 in Little Rock on the last play of the game on an 18-yard catch by Tony Jones from quarterback Bret Stafford. Midway through the 2005 season, it was still the only time UT has won a game with a touchdown on the final play.

With the Longhorns trailing 14-10 and a field goal not an option, McWilliams called a timeout to set up the last play. He, Stafford, and UT offensive coordinator John Mize decided on a pass play.

Stafford said, "Coach, I believe if I can sprint one way and throw back to Tony on a quick post, that's the best way to get it in there."

McWilliams told him to play his hunch. And Stafford did what he said he could do. He sprinted to the right and threw back to the other side of the field.

"That kind of got [Arkansas defensive back Steve] Atwater out of the middle," McWilliams said. "When he threw to Tony, Tony's back was to me. One of the other defensive backs just knocked the crud out of him. What happened—if you look at it on the film—their secondary got too deep. They were back four or five yards in the end zone. That let Tony get underneath."

Away Goes Jones

That catch against Arkansas seemed to energize Tony Jones. As a senior, in 1988, Jones led Texas in receiving with 42 catches for 838 yards (a 20-yard average per catch). During the course of his career from 1986 to 1989 he had seven 100-yard receiving games, four alone in 1988.

"Tony Jones, up until that time, of course, had that great speed, but he was an average receiver," McWilliams said. "He would catch some and he would drop some. After he caught that pass [against Arkansas], I don't remember him dropping any balls the rest of his career. Sometimes there is a play which makes a difference in a player."

Wild Game at Astrodome

In the 1987 game against Houston at the Astrodome, UT held a 34-20 lead in the second quarter. But eventually Houston ran an NCAA-record four intercepted passes back for touchdowns.

Johnny Jackson had an NCAA individual record three interception runbacks for touchdowns (31, 53, 97 yards). Houston also started completing passes with its Run-and-Shoot offense in a stunning 60-40 victory over Texas.

"We have them down and we lost [Bret] Stafford," McWilliams said. "He was the only quarterback we had. He hits one of those spots down there in the Astrodome where the concrete is showing up off the field and screws up his elbow. We ended up losing. And we couldn't stop that little fullback draw."

Houston followed the 1987 victory over Texas with 66-15 and 47-9 triumphs over the Longhorns the following two seasons.

The Last Bluebonnet Bowl

Texas, with a 6-5 record in McWilliams's first season, accepted a bid to the Bluebonnet Bowl in Houston. It would wind up being the

David McWilliams was a player, an assistant coach, and a head coach for the Longhorns. *Cotton Bowl Athletic Association*

final Bluebonnet Bowl game when only 23,282 fans showed up to see Texas beat Pittsburgh 32-27.

Texas's earlier 60-40 loss to Houston played into this financial fiasco. The last-place UT fans wanted to watch a game was in Houston against anybody.

"I was in an unusual position in 1987," said Ted Nance, the former Houston sports information director. "I was executive director of the Bluebonnet Bowl. I went to the UH-Texas game in the Astrodome thinking Texas would be the team for our bowl. UH was going nowhere. UH scored 31 points in the fourth quarter. We invited Texas anyway, which proved to be a mistake."

Texas sold only 5,000 tickets of its 12,500 allotment. And the Bluebonnet Bowl, already financially strapped, closed its doors when it couldn't pay off the teams.

The Sabotage of the 1988 Season?

Eric Metcalf was UT's leading rusher during the 1987 and 1988 seasons when he gained more than 2,000 yards on the ground and scored 18 touchdowns during the two seasons. But he was held out of the 1988 season opener against BYU.

"I think that really disrupted our season," McWilliams said. "What had happened was Eric had gotten money to go to summer school, but he didn't go because of the Olympics [in South Korea]. But he didn't turn the money back in that time. When we found out about it, he paid the money back. We reported it. We had seen in similar situations where the player had done community service and not been penalized any games."

As 19th-ranked UT boarded an airplane to go to Provo, Metcalf was not allowed to board. And by the time McWilliams got to the team hotel in Provo, he had gotten word that the NCAA had suspended Metcalf for one game.

Some UT players wanted to tape Metcalf's number on their shoes and/or uniforms, but that was against NCAA rules as well.

BYU won 47-6.

"We start the game, and on the opening play they throw a touchdown pass over Mark Berry," McWilliams said.

"It started bad. And it stayed bad. I knew Saturday before the game all [the players] were talking about was Metcalf. I could just tell we were losing them on that game. It was really hard, even for the coaches. I don't know that Eric would have made a difference, but he certainly would have made a difference in our attitude."

Texas struggled to a 4-7 season.

Gardere Happens on the Scene

If there was a bright spot in UT's second straight losing season in 1989 (5-6) and third in four years, it was the development of freshman quarterback Peter Gardere, who had redshirted the previous season.

"We were rotating three quarterbacks, and actually, Gardere was our third quarterback," McWilliams said. "We played all three of them. And it seemed like every time we got him into a game, he moved the chains. I remember that we were 80 yards out and he told players in the huddle, 'Hey, we are going to move the ball and score and win this thing.' And that gave them confidence."

Narrow Escape

In 1989, Texas had a close call against Rice 31-30. UT (1-2) was coming off a 16-12 loss to Penn State.

Texas had a first-and-goal at the Rice nine. But after three plays UT had advanced only to the four-yard line. Gardere, on the fourth-down play, rolled right on the option and was headed to the end zone. He was tackled before he reached it. But he lunged forward and knocked over the pylon to tie the score 30-30.

"We got screwed," said Rice's Matt Sign. "He hits the pylon and all of sudden [the official] raises his hands."

Wayne Clements then kicked the extra point for the win with more than five minutes remaining in the game.

"I just started running," Gardere said. "I tried to get to the pylon. I hit it. And that is all that counts. Maybe somebody knocked it over. It counted."

Mark Berry intercepted Rice quarterback Donald Hollas on the first play of the Owls' final drive.

"It certainly was questionable," McWilliams said of Gardere's touchdown. "And I could have understood if I had been on the other side."

Shock the Nation, They Did

In 1990, Texas was on its "Shock the Nation Tour." McWilliams had read a bank advertisement that said "Whatever it Takes" and also had adopted that slogan.

Players came to McWilliams, told him they were tired of losing, and began 6 a.m. workouts.

The defining moment may have occurred in a 45-24 victory over Houston in UT's eighth game of the season.

Houston entered the game as the No. 3-ranked team in the nation. Texas was No. 14. Houston had averaged 58 points a game over the last three games versus Texas.

"I think that was the high point, as far as the electricity in the stadium," McWilliams said. "I think Mack Brown has it that way now, every game. That was the first time in a long time."

UT defensive coordinator Leon Fuller and McWilliams did not deviate as other teams had from their basic 4-3 defense. Fuller went over the game plan before the game on television, much to the shock of the announcers.

With the bump and run, Fuller said, "we took away their short passes where they had made so many yards and forced them to throw down field." This also allowed UT's defense to zero in on Houston quarterback David Klingler, who wound up throwing four interceptions. UT's victory propelled it to a 10-1 regular-season record and a Cotton Bowl berth.

"That game was the most exciting I have ever been involved with," Gardere said. "It was similar to the OU game at the Cotton Bowl."

Dramatic Win in College Station

The final game of the 1990 season came down to a two-point conversion play.

With four minutes to play, Texas A&M coach R.C. Slocum didn't believe his team would get the ball back after Bucky Richardson had raced 32 yards to narrow the score to 28-27 in favor of Texas. Had he kicked the extra point, Slocum might have been settling for a tie, because there was no overtime in that era.

Slocum's call was a dive option play. Richardson was pressured and had nowhere to go. He pitched the ball to Aggies running back Darren Lewis, who was stopped by Longhorns defensive back Mark Berry. Texas won to finish the regular season 10-1 and gain a berth in the Cotton Bowl.

Slocum had called a timeout to set up the two-point conversion attempt. CBS cameras were so close to the Texas A&M coaches that the audio could be heard of the play call. Later Richardson said he almost called an audible when he saw that the Texas defense was stacked where the play was going.

"To start with, we didn't see it because there was a commercial going on," McWilliams said.

"I wish we had seen it…. We thought they would come out in an unbalanced line and run that option to the short two-man side. Leon Fuller said he was going to run red-dog [blitzing from the strong side and weak side]. And maybe if they had run that option we could have gotten to the ball quicker and gotten somebody to come up on it. So that was what he called."

UT linebacker Brian Jones broke through between the guard and tackle. Richardson had to pitch. The UT safety came up and took on the blocker. So that left Mark Berry with a receiver man-to-man, but he came up to take on the ball carrier.

"'What if it had been a halfback pass?' I asked Mark after the game," McWilliams said. "'Why did you leave that receiver?'

"He said, 'Ah, Coach, I knew they were running it.'

"I said, 'I am glad you did.'

"He hit Lewis about five yards behind the line of scrimmage. He made a perfect tackle. I was telling someone that was the same guy [Berry] that on the first play of his college career they threw an 80-yard touchdown pass over him at BYU."

Burn Those Stories

In 1991, Bobby Cannon, at the time the oldest UT football letterman alive at age 94, sent disparaging letters and newspaper clippings he had collected to head coach David McWilliams and quarterbacks Peter Gardere and Jimmy Saxton.

Texas's 1991 team opened the season with losses to Mississippi State (13-6) and Auburn (14-10).

Cannon told them to begin a stack and to put the pile in a garbage can and set it afire in the locker room before the Rice game. UT beat Rice 28-7 to snap the two-game losing streak.

The Last Go-Around with Arkansas

In 1991 Arkansas beat Texas 14-13 in the last regular-season game between the two teams as members of the old Southwest Conference.

The regular-season series would not be renewed until the 2003 season in Austin. Texas kickers missed an extra point and a 39-yard field goal attempt in the fourth quarter.

Arkansas left the SWC for the Southeastern Conference and would play eight conference games each season, making it difficult to schedule a game with Texas given the tough SEC conference foes.

"It's just a change of life," UT athletic director DeLoss Dodds said in 1991. "It wasn't our decision. It was their decision [to go to the SEC]."

But UT legend Darrell Royal was sorry to see it end.

"I wish we could keep playing, but that is the way love goes," Royal said wistfully in 1991. He had a 15-5 record versus Arkansas, losing three of five games by a total of nine points from 1964 to 1966.

Arkansas did beat Texas 27-6 in the first college football game played in the new millennium on January 1, 2000, in the Cotton Bowl. But that was the only game between the two teams between 1991 and 2003.

"The game has always been more important to Arkansas than it has been to Texas, except for a period of six, seven, eight, or nine years when Darrell and I were coaching," said Arkansas coach Frank Broyles, who had a 5-14 record versus Texas.

McWilliams's Downward Spiral

Following Texas's 1990 SWC championship season, Texas had eight players selected in the 1991 NFL draft. That was the most since the 18-player draft of 1984.

That loss of talent and problems in the kicking game meant another losing season in 1991 (5-6) and the end of the relatively short McWilliams era.

"We couldn't even kick an extra point in the Arkansas game, and we missed two field goals inside the 20-yard line," McWilliams said of a 14-13 loss to the Razorbacks. "[Kicker] Jason Ziegler from McKinney tore his hamstring, his whole thigh muscle. I felt we lost four games that year because we were not able to kick a field goal."

In five years, McWilliams had two winning seasons and compiled a 31-26 overall record.

"This was my school," McWilliams said. "There was no amount of pressure from anybody more than what I wanted the Longhorns to do well. So I felt maybe it was time to get someone else in here. I was disappointed I hadn't done a better job in the five years I had been here. I am proud of the fact I recruited good kids and they got degrees. But it was time for someone else to come in. And I am not embarrassed about it. I am not upset. I fought as hard as I could to get this thing going. And I didn't get it done."

Assessing Mackovic

After the end of the David McWilliams era, there was a roundtable to discuss the prospects for UT's new coach.

"It was alumni, some of the players, and other coaches, and they said what they thought they would like in a coach," said Gardere. "Kiki DeAyala [Texas player from 1980 to 1982] played for the Kansas City Chiefs and said no player on the team liked John Mackovic. The players didn't want to play for him. I remember that was the first thing I had heard about that. But I think the decision already had been made to hire him."

Changing of the Guard

Gardere played three seasons for David McWilliams and his senior year (1992) for coach John Mackovic.

"They were two different personalities," Gardere said. "McWilliams was a good ol' boy and played at Texas. He mainly let his assistants do the coaching. Mackovic was totally different. He wanted to do his own thing. Tradition was not that important. He wanted to start his own regime. The first year he took the team picture in white, instead of orange…. He was very hands-on. He wanted to call the plays and be very involved."

Gardere said his starting quarterback job was in jeopardy every week of the season.

"He picked a starter each week," said Gardere, who remained the starter. "We charted every play [in practice]. You had a little added pressure you don't need…. I really liked John Mackovic. It was tough his first year. He just wanted to put a fire under everybody. He wanted you to know who was boss."

Sherill's Flap with Bevo

Before Mississippi State's 28-10 victory over Texas on September 5, 1992, in coach John Mackovic's first game as the UT coach, Mississippi State coach Jackie Sherrill had a steer castrated in front of his players at a practice.

Sherrill said the whole story came up the week before the Texas game when he asked his players what a steer was and none of them knew. Sherrill said the castration was done for two reasons: education and motivation.

A steer is a castrated male of the cattle family. The Longhorn is a steer. So there was some role-playing there.

Sherrill said the calf's owner was going to perform the castration whether or not the Mississippi State players watched.

TCU Winning Streak Ends

Texas had not lost to TCU since a 24-17 defeat during the 1967 season. That 24-game winning streak ended in 1992 against TCU 23-14 in John Mackovic's first season.

"That hurt," quarterback Peter Gardere said. "They had prepared for us all year. One of the TCU players, meeting him a couple of years later, told me they had stolen our signals."

Mackovic's first season ended with a 6-5 record, only a victory improvement over McWilliams's 5-6 record in 1991. And in 1993, the UT record slipped to 5-5-1.

1994: Pivotal Year

Texas won four of its first five games, including a 17-10 victory over Oklahoma. But in a rare Sunday night game, Texas lost to Rice 19-17 in front of a national ESPN audience.

It was Rice's first victory over UT since a 20-17 defeat in 1965. Texas had won 28 straight in the series.

"Am I shocked?" Mackovic said after the game. "No, I have been coaching for 30 years."

UT was missing seven players who had been suspended by Mackovic for staying out late. Among them were star receivers Michael Adams and Lovell Pinkney.

Mackovic's Mysterious Condition

Mackovic later revealed he hadn't been quite right in that Rice game. He had suffered a concussion on the sideline when Tony Brackens and Tre Thomas bowled him over 15 days earlier during a 34-31 loss at Colorado.

Mackovic suffered cuts to his chin and elbow and also sustained post-concussion syndrome.

"It was like I was watching the picture from the outside instead of being on the inside of the picture," Mackovic said.

Texas managed to salvage a 7-4 regular season and then edged North Carolina and coach Mack Brown 35-31 in the Sun Bowl.

As Time Ran out

One of the most exciting endings for any Texas football game during any season was the Longhorns' 17-16 victory over No. 14 Virginia in 1995 in Austin. Coming after a disappointing 24-24 tie with Oklahoma, the exhilarating victory over the Cavaliers served as a springboard for a six-game winning streak and a Southwest Conference title in the last season of the league.

Phil Dawson's 50-yard field goal as time expired was the difference in the game. It was the first time a UT placekicker had won a game on the last play. And it was the first time the Longhorns had won a game at home on the last play of a contest.

"I never really thought we were going to lose the game," Mackovic said. "I just didn't know how we were going to win it."

On fourth and 10, UT quarterback James Brown completed a 12-yard pass to keep the drive alive. He intentionally grounded the ball to stop the clock and then scrambled 11 yards to the Virginia 33 with three seconds remaining.

Running back Ricky Williams had to hide his eyes before turning to watch as the ball sailed through the uprights. It was the 700th victory in school history.

The Imposter

Upon completion of the 1995 season, SWC champion Texas accepted a bid to the Sugar Bowl. A 28-10 loss to Virginia Tech was overshadowed by the imposter defensive back "Joel Ron McKelvey."

The imposter had played in all 11 of Texas's 1995 regular-season games. His real name was Ron Weaver. A 30-year-old, Weaver had already played six years of college football in California, four at junior colleges and two at Sacramento State. A paper in Salinas, California, *The Californian,* was doing stories on hometown players in bowl games when it discovered the discrepancy in Weaver's identity two days before the Sugar Bowl game.

The Californian reported that Weaver was working on a book about the scandals of college football, which he apparently was helping to create. He left New Orleans before his teammates or coaches could ask him about his imposter's role.

Notre Dame's Squeaker

In 1996, for the first time in 44 years, the Fighting Irish would play in Austin. And it was a matchup of top-10 teams that went down to the final play of the game.

Ricky Williams scored on a spin move near the goal line to push Texas ahead 24-17 with 10:53 remaining in the game.

Notre Dame tied the score after a James Brown interception. But instead of giving the ball to Williams for a winning drive, Mackovic went to the passing game. With the score tied at 24-24, the UT offense bogged down.

"We were running the ball up and down the field; then we wanted to get unpredictable," said UT running backs coach Bucky Godboldt.

Mackovic said he was playing for a field goal. But Williams was used only twice. Notre Dame kicked a 39-yard field goal with no time remaining to win the game 27-24.

Prepping for Nebraska

By winning 51-15 over Texas A&M, UT qualified for the first Big 12 title game in St. Louis against Nebraska. The defending national champion Cornhuskers had lost only one game all season at Arizona State. And they were three-touchdown favorites to beat 7-4 Texas and advance to a third straight national title game.

Before the game, UT quarterback James Brown pulled a Joe Namath. He predicted the Longhorns would beat Nebraska by three touchdowns. Brown knew what he was talking about. And, like Joe Namath, he delivered with 353 yards passing in UT's 37-27 upset victory.

"I can't remember a game since I have been here at Nebraska [20 years] where we have had that many big plays against us," said Nebraska defensive coordinator Charlie McBride.

Roll Left

The 1996 championship game would be remembered for one play: Roll Left. It was the most daring call in coach John Mackovic's

In 1996, quarterback James Brown predicted the Longhorns would defeat defending national champs Nebraska in the Big 12 title game. He delivered on his promise, as he passed for 353 yards and UT won 37-27. *Todd Warshaw/Getty Images*

tenure at Texas. But being daring would secure a victory, a Big 12 title and a berth in the Fiesta Bowl.

Texas, clinging to a 30-27 lead, faced a fourth-and-inches at its own 28 with 2:48 remaining in the game.

"I was prepared to punt," Mackovic said. "But when they stretched the chain and we needed two inches, I thought, heck, if you are going to be a champion, you have to go for it. You have to seize the day."

Everybody, including Nebraska's famed "Blackshirt" defense, was expecting a sneak by quarterback James Brown. Nebraska coach Tom Osborne also expected UT might be trying to draw the Cornhuskers offsides.

Instead, Nebraska saw the riverboat gambler in Mackovic. Brown was to run if he saw a hole, but he also was to fake a handoff to Priest Holmes and throw if there was no hole. If the defense bit, as it often did on the fake to Holmes, there would be a receiver wide open.

And there was.

Brown, hounded by roverback Mike Mintner, lifted a pass to Derek Lewis, a sophomore tight end, who caught the ball at the UT 43 and rambled down to the Cornhusker 11 before he was caught.

Texas scored on the next play.

"We knew what [Mackovic] was going to call," Brown said. "There really wasn't a doubt in anybody's mind. It was Roll Left. You can't stop that play if we execute it. The defense doesn't have enough people to cover it."

Applewhite's Recruitment

UT quarterback Major Applewhite, from Baton Rouge, Louisiana, was named by his father Larry, who was a huge Alabama fan. Applewhite was named after Major Ogilvie, who led Alabama to national titles in 1978 and 1979. Applewhite attended Alabama's football camps starting as a third grader and for years had a passion to attend Alabama, but was never recruited by the Crimson Tide.

Instead he was recruited by Texas A&M offensive coordinator Steve Ensminger, who was originally from Baton Rouge and knew of Applewhite's abilities.

Because his high school team ran the ball a lot, Applewhite wanted to go to a school that threw the ball, and he believed A&M would under Ensminger. At Baton Rouge's Catholic High,

Applewhite was part of the Major-Minor offense, with running back Travis Minor, who would later star at Florida State.

But after Applewhite actually committed to Texas A&M in 1996, he un-committed the next week after A&M coach R.C. Slocum fired Ensminger and two other assistants in a shakeup of the Aggies staff. Texas beat A&M that season 51-15, and Applewhite believed his reversal of decisions had been justified.

See, Told You So

Former Texas men's basketball coach Tom Penders was one of the most colorful and unpredictable coaches the Longhorns have ever had. He took the 'Horns to eight NCAA Tournaments in his 10 years as coach from 1988-1989 through the 1997-1998 season. But during much of his tenure, the Longhorns football team struggled while the basketball team prospered.

When Penders became coach in the spring of 1988, David McWilliams was the Longhorns' football coach and was followed after the 1991 season by John Mackovic, whose last season as UT's head football coach was 1997. Following the 1997 season, Mack Brown became UT's third head football coach in Penders's tenure during his final season at the school.

Along with a recruit, Penders attended UT's humiliating 66-3 loss to UCLA in Austin during Mackovic's final season in 1997. But Penders could always make the best of a bad situation.

"See," Penders told the player, "I told you Texas was a basketball school."

The UCLA Fallout

The 66-3 loss to UCLA may have been the worst game to watch in Austin in modern Longhorns history. Texas committed eight turnovers, which UCLA turned into six touchdowns. Five of those miscues occurred in the second quarter alone and turned into 28 UCLA points. Six of UCLA's 14 drives started in UT territory.

It couldn't have come at a worse time for marketing purposes. UT was trying to sell 50 new suites on the east side of Memorial Stadium.

Mack Rankin, a powerful Dallas alum, already had bought one of the new suites on the west side. He posted a sign on his suite at halftime of the UCLA game, in which the Bruins led 38-0. "Skybox for sale or rent," it read.

Texas would struggle to a 4-7 record. And after a 27-16 loss to Texas A&M, Mackovic was fired.

CHAPTER ELEVEN

Ricky Williams

Ricky's Recruiting Visit

Ricky Williams, from San Diego, was recruited by UCLA, USC, and San Diego State, but he fell in love with Austin when he made his recruiting trip to Austin before signing with the Longhorns in the winter of 1995. Williams liked the weather, all the big linemen he could run behind, the people, and the fact that Earl Campbell played for Texas and won the Heisman Trophy in 1977.

"I think Californians have this feel for the University of Texas," said former UT running backs coach Bucky Godbolt. "I don't know what it is, but Californians seem to think it is a special place. The weather may have something to do with it.

"I think what intrigued Ricky was Earl Campbell, who was big and strong and real similar to Ricky," Godbolt continued. "[Ricky] said he was going to come to Texas if he liked the people, the weather, the atmosphere. When he came to Texas he had an outstanding visit. Through all of that, he gave his word."

The Stiff Arm

One of the things that made Ricky Williams an effective runner during his years at Texas (1995-1998) was a stiff arm he developed under the tutelage of Godbolt. Each week Godbolt had a

sled out working running backs. Starting with Williams his freshman year, he developed the stiff arm.

"[The reason] why [Williams] got a lot of extra yards was the stiff arm," Godbolt said. "We worked on it for two years. Nobody uses it anymore. Ricky got a lot of extra yards turning a [tackler] sideways, using it as a tool. It was an art. Every day that was part of the workout. They would get on the seven-man sled and hit it on a certain level. They got tired of it. But in a game they all could turn a guy sideways."

UT sports information director John Bianco kept a special Ricky Williams statistic: yards after contact. Williams averaged 84.5 of his 136.5 yards a game during his UT career after contact.

Williams: The Blocker

In UT's stunning 37-27 victory over Nebraska in the Big 12 Conference's first title game in 1996, Ricky Williams was used as a blocker against ends Grant Wistrom and Jared Tomich, not as a runner.

UT running back Priest Holmes gained 120 yards and scored three touchdowns in the upset.

"[Williams] made about 20 big blocks in that game," Godbolt said. "I think it was the best game he ever played. He blocked All-Americans on every play. He picked one up and body-slammed him. He blocked the entire game one on one and he enjoyed this game."

Godbolt said he told Williams on the sidelines they were sorry they weren't springing him free. "But he was having a great time. He would say, 'Did you see that?' [after he made a block]. At the point of attack he was pummeling those guys," Godbolt recalled.

Williams: The Decoy

Williams was the decoy in the longest pass play in Texas history (midway through the 2005 season) during a 34-3 victory over Oklahoma in the 1998 season.

Quarterback Major Applewhite connected with Wane McGarity for a 97-yard completion early in the third quarter.

Applewhite faked a handoff to Williams and completed the play-action pass to McGarity.

"I think that was the turning point in the season," said UT offensive coordinator Greg Davis. "We said, 'Look, we have confidence we will protect from the three-yard line, and Major will take care of the ball.' That was probably the turning point of the season, we could beat you either way."

Perplexing Use

Entering a game against Missouri during the 1997 season, Texas had won 22 straight games when it had rushed for 200 yards or more as a team. That streak ended when the Longhorns lost to Missouri 37-29 in the sixth game of the season.

Williams carried 23 times for 235 yards and became the first UT back to gain 200 or more yards rushing in consecutive games. Against Missouri, he averaged 10.2 yards a carry. But mysteriously, quarterback James Brown was firing away in the final quarter and completed just 15 of 40 passes for the game. UT only ran the ball 30 times.

Williams became the first UT back to rush for more than 200 yards in a losing cause.

After the game, coach John Mackovic told reporters he did not run Williams more because he was tired. Relayed this statement by a member of the UT sports information staff, Williams hurled his helmet down in disgust.

Did You Know?

Ricky Willliams finished his junior season with 1,893 yards rushing and was better in nearly every statistical category than Earl Campbell was when "The Tyler Rose" won the Heisman Trophy in 1977.

Trouble was Williams's team finished just 4-7, and Campbell's team went unbeaten before losing to Notre Dame in the Cotton Bowl.

Campbell had 1,744 yards rushing. Williams beat Campbell in carries, yards per carry, yards per game, and rushing touchdowns.

Campbell did have more 100-yard rushing games (10 to Williams's eight), but Williams had more 200-yard rushing games (six to Campbell's two).

Yet Williams wasn't even invited to New York City for the Heisman Show because he finished fifth in the balloting behind Michigan's Charles Woodson (the winner), Tennessee's Peyton Manning, Washington State's Ryan Leaf, and Marshall's Randy Moss.

"I was heartbroken," Williams told the *Houston Chronicle.* "I thought I at least deserved a little recognition for the season I had. I think I put up numbers to be mentioned, to be a candidate.... I think I was the best player in college football."

Connecting with Mack Brown

After the disappointing junior season (4-7) and the firing of John Mackovic, Williams had a big decision to make: whether or not to remain at Texas for his senior season. New UT coach Mack Brown said he knew who his biggest recruit would be: Ricky Williams.

Brown said he met with Williams three times, "and he got a little warmer every time." Williams had concerns about discipline on the team, the kind of offense, and whether or not Texas would have a chance to win. Brown also had to deal with Williams's dreadlocks.

"Generally, we had a standing rule," Brown said about hair. "We wanted all of our guys to present themselves in a position where they could get a job out of college. So our hair rule had been they need to wear their hair like they are going to interview for a job. In Ricky's situation, he interviews for a job every Saturday. So he was going to get work. So it wasn't as big an issue to me."

Williams was given assurances by Brown that he would be the hub of the offense. On January 8, 1998, Williams announced he would stay. He signed a $2.8 million insurance policy in case of injury his senior season.

Wearing out Numbers

Ricky Williams actually wore three numbers during his college career at Texas: Nos. 11, 34, and 37.

He began his career at UT wearing No. 11 the first three seasons. He wanted to wear No. 34, the number he wore at Patrick Henry High School in San Diego, because he idolized Bo Jackson.

UT linebacker Tremaine Brown wore No. 34 when Williams first arrived in Austin. Brown quit the team later that fall, but then head coach John Mackovic did not allow number changes.

After Mackovic was fired following the 1997 season, Brown allowed Williams to take over No. 34 for his senior year; Williams's No. 11 went to quarterback Major Applewhite.

Williams's third number worn at UT was for one game against Oklahoma during his senior season. Williams wore No. 37 in honor of the legendary Doak Walker in the game at the Cotton Bowl, "the House that Doak Built." Walker was a consensus All-American for SMU from 1947 to 1949.

UT won the game 34-3. The Walker family was presented with the jersey by Williams, who rushed for 139 yards and also had a 78-yard touchdown run called back by penalty, in an emotional ceremony afterward.

The No. 37 ran wild that day. The Walker family sat on row 37. The final score added up to 37 points. The Texas lotto that weekend was for $37 million. One of the Walker daughters bought 37 tickets, but failed to win.

A UT Record Day for Williams

Midway through the 2005 season, Ricky Williams still held the UT record for most yards gained in a game—350 yards gained against Iowa State during the 1998 season in a 54-33 UT victory. The legendary Doak Walker (Williams had won the Doak Walker Award as a junior and would again as a senior) had passed away at the age of 71 the previous week.

UT petitioned the NCAA to allow Williams to wear the No. 37 decal on his helmet against Iowa State. It was permitted, and it served as great inspiration for Williams. Through the 2002 season,

Ricky Williams stuck around for his senior year after hitting it off with new coach Mack Brown, who allowed Williams to keep his dreadlocks.
Brian Bahr/Getty Images

the 350 yards still ranked as the 14th best single-game total for a rusher in NCAA Division 1-A history.

UT offensive coordinator Greg Davis remembers Williams was a man possessed during this game at Memorial Stadium. Davis called the isolation play on third down and long and basically had conceded the set of downs.

"I remember that play specifically," Davis said. "We were going into the wind. I had started to call a pass. Then I thought I would run the isolation play. The quarter would be over [and UT could punt with the wind at its back]. And he goes 68 yards for a touchdown."

Mack's Little Game

Texas coach Mack Brown had this little game he played with his rules about being late. They applied to everyone but Ricky Williams, who perpetually was late for the team bus and meetings.

Brown had a meeting with Williams and his position coach and told Williams: "I can't kick you off the team or fire you," Brown said and he turned and pointed to the position coach, "but I will fire you if he is not on time."

Williams turned to his position coach and asked: "Would he do that?"

The position coach nodded.

Brown, for Ricky's senior season, operated on "Ricky Time." He would call the position coach and ask when Ricky would be down for the team bus or team meeting or meal. Brown wouldn't show up until Williams had already arrived.

Ricky Williams's Fill-in

Sam Nicola, the director of Touchdown Club of Columbus (Ohio), wanted to honor Ricky Williams as the club's running back of the year. But when Williams couldn't attend, and Williams's mother, Sandy, passed on attending the February banquet in 1999, Nicola still wanted a warm Texas body in the house.

So he called UT sports information director John Bianco and asked if freshman quarterback Major Applewhite could attend.

Applewhite had had a sensational rookie season and thus won the College Freshman of the Year Award created by Nicola especially for the occasion. Applewhite and his father attended.

Ending Nebraska's Streak

Nebraska had a 47-game home-field winning streak when Texas and Ricky Williams went to Lincoln on October 31, 1998. And what a Halloween evening it was when the unranked Longhorns came away with a stunning 20-16 victory over the No. 7-ranked Cornhuskers.

Nebraska's 47-game home-field winning streak still ranked as the fifth longest in Division I-A history through the 2002 season. Nebraska hadn't lost at home since the 1991 season, nor had they lost to an unranked team at home since Missouri in 1978.

"We went through the walk-through [in Lincoln, the day before the game]," said UT associate athletic director for external affairs, Chris Plonsky. "And there was a calmness about our football team which was really bizarre. Our guys were confident. They weren't zealous. But they were really steady. I think Mack thought we could give them a game. And if we could stay in it long enough, we could win it. And I think on Ricky [Williams's] first two or three runs, he got yardage and he bumped a couple of guys off. He made it evident to the world he was going to be hard to bring down."

Williams Applauded

Nebraska fans are some of the best in college football. And when Ricky Williams rushed for 150 yards in leading his team to the 20-16 victory, they applauded him after the game.

So did then Nebraska defensive coordinator Charlie McBride. It was a Heisman Trophy-clinching performance as far as the veteran McBride was concerned. Williams's 150 yards were the most by an opposing back in Lincoln since Oklahoma State's Barry Sanders gained 189 in a 63-42 Oklahoma State loss to the Cornhuskers in 1988. And that season Sanders won the Heisman Trophy.

Ricky Williams broke Tony Dorsett's I-A career rushing record against Texas A&M in 1998. *Cotton Bowl Athletic Association*

"The guy is something special," McBride said. "The two best guys we have played against are Barry Sanders and Ricky Williams. If he doesn't win the Heisman Trophy, college football has something wrong with it. It's the politically right thing to do. He's such a powerful kid and has such great balance. And you hear other things you like—not football things. But his work habits, him staying for his senior year when he could have left and made a lot of money. All that adds up to is character. He's a special player."

No Target Practice for Cornhuskers

Before Texas's 20-16 victory over Nebraska, Cornhuskers defenders said they were going to have target practice on Ricky Williams. But in a surprising move, Williams said: "I'm going to make them the target when I get the ball."

UT coach Mack Brown was rather surprised his star running back was so vocal.

"I asked Ricky why he said that," Brown said. "He said, 'I want our team to be confident. If they don't think I am confident, then they won't be confident.'"

After the game, Williams told reporters: "Nebraska said they were going to put a target on me. So I didn't think I would see any holes. But some of the holes were gaping."

In fact, Williams did, indeed, make unsuspecting Nebraska players his prey on the field. He made a touchdown-saving tackle in the third quarter on an interception of a Major Applewhite pass. And he also blocked a blitzing linebacker later to allow Applewhite to complete a big pass.

Setting the Record

Ricky Williams broke the NCAA Division I-A rushing record of Tony Dorsett, a record that had stood for 22 years, at 10:47 a.m. on Friday, November 27, 1998. He went 60 yards on L King Zin 53 at Memorial Stadium in Austin.

Brent Musburger on ABC television made the call on the historic run during a 26-24 victory against Texas A&M.

"He's offset a little bit to the left. Eleven yards from tying the record.... Williams breaks the hole. Williams, hello record book.... Ricky Williams runs to the Hall of Fame!

"Cutback. Ricky Williams touchdown! ...60 yards and the record is his. He did it in dramatic fashion. And a standing ovation for the king of the rushers..."

Williams carried a career-high 44 times for 259 yards to smash Dorsett's career rushing record. A year later Wisconsin's Ron Dayne would break Williams's record. But the performance clinched the Heisman Trophy for Williams, who had finished fifth in the balloting the previous year.

Heisman Runaway

Ricky Williams won the Heisman Trophy in a landside. His closest competition was Kansas State quarterback Michael Bishop. And Bishop was a distant second, trailing Williams 2,355 votes to

792. Williams won by the fourth-largest margin in the history of the award.

Williams received 714 first-place votes, the third most in the history of the award. He swept the voting in all six regions, with at least a 200-point margin in each sector.

CHAPTER TWELVE

Mack of a Different Kind

Getting Mack Brown

Mack Brown had made North Carolina a top-10 program. He had forged eight straight winning seasons in Chapel Hill and had taken the team to bowls in his final six seasons there. So he made the decision to go to Texas with mixed feelings after the 1997 season.

"We had 10 years of time and energy and commitment put into that program," Brown said. "And the program was in the top 10 the last two years.

"Walking in to talk to that North Carolina team on that day [I was leaving] was the hardest thing I ever had to do athletically because I had been in the home of every young man at that school."

After John Mackovic was fired, Texas was interviewing Brown and Northwestern coach Gary Barnett at the same time. But Brown certainly fit the Texas profile as a charismatic coach who could relate to alumni.

Recruiting Ricky

Brown said his biggest recruit at Texas would be Ricky Williams. He had to convince the star running back to stay for his senior season. After several meetings with Brown and some bending of Brown's personal appearance rules for players, Williams decided he would have a chance to win the Heisman Trophy in 1998.

He and Brown clicked. But Brown didn't know if Williams could win the Heisman Trophy or gain the 2,000 yards needed to make that dream come true.

"He is as good as I had ever seen," Brown said. "But we were inexperienced at quarterback and receiver. I thought 'There is no way in the world he can get 2,000 yards rushing.' So when they asked me if he could, I told them every defense in America is going to key on him. And they did. And then he still got more than 2,000 yards."

Applewhite Survives

Speaking of young quarterbacks...

In that 1998 season, Texas started 1-2 in Mack Brown's first season after Kansas State defeated Texas 48-7. Freshman Major Applewhite completed 16 of 37 passes and threw two interceptions against the Wildcats.

At one point, linebacker Jeff Kelly intercepted one of Applewhite's passes and returned it 17 yards for a touchdown.

A Kansas State player yelled in Applewhite's ear, "We've got you rattled!"

A Kansas State fan was even worse, e-mailing Applewhite later, "Great game, Opie. Too bad the rest of the team played like Aunt Bea."

But Applewhite, along with Ricky Williams, would rally Texas to a 9-3 record, including a victory at Nebraska, one over A&M, and a triumph over Mississippi State in the Cotton Bowl.

Applewhite's Nebraska-Killer Passes

Some of the top plays in Applewhite's career were passes he threw against the Cornhuskers during two regular-season games in 1998 and 1999.

In the 1998 upset of Nebraska in Lincoln, Applewhite's clutch two-yard pass on third down to Wane McGarity with 2:47 remaining clinched a 20-16 victory for UT and ended Nebraska's 47-game home-field winning streak. That touchdown was set up by Applewhite's third-

and-21 throw to Bryan White, which went for 37 yards and kept the
drive alive.

In a 24-20 Texas victory over Nebraska in 1999 in Austin,
Applewhite threw for 213 yards and two touchdowns against a
No. 3-ranked Cornhuskers defense. He was good on eight of nine
passes in the second half, including both touchdowns.

Allen's Hex on Texas

In 1999, Kansas State defeated Texas 35-17 in Austin as the
Wildcats' David Allen had his way with the Longhorns' special
teams once again.

Texas led Kansas State 14-9 in the third quarter when Allen
returned a punt 74 yards without being touched. It was the seventh
punt return for a touchdown by Allen in his career and put the
Wildcats ahead to stay.

Allen also had a 93-yard punt return for a touchdown against
Texas in a 1998 Wildcats victory in Manhattan, Kansas.

"It was a mistake," Texas coach Mack Brown told reporters after
the 1999 game of a 48-yard punt by Ryan Long. "We had been kicking
away from [Allen] all day. But this time we missed by five yards."

The Bonfire Game

The final UT game of the 1999 regular season had somber
overtones. In the days leading up to the game, 12 Texas A&M
students died when the traditional Aggies bonfire collapsed.

At halftime, the Texas Longhorn Band, in honor of the 12
fallen Texas A&M students, played "Amazing Grace" and "Taps." It
opted not to play the Texas fight song.

Texas also cancelled its annual "Texas A&M Hex Rally" for the
A&M game and held a memorial service for the fallen Texas A&M
students. Some Texas fans and players were even singing "The Aggie
War Hymn" at the game.

There were blood drives in Austin to help the wounded.

The Texas A&M sports information department granted 712
credentials. And the game was played before a state record crowd of
86,128 at the time. Texas A&M won 20-16 to end a tough week.

A&M Pranks

On the day of the 1999 Texas A&M game in College Station, Mack Brown, offensive coordinator Greg Davis, defensive coordinator Carl Reese, and several players received calls at 4 a.m. at the Ramada Inn. The numbers had been posted on the Internet.

For a 6:15 a.m. breakfast, the cook at the Ramada Inn restaurant didn't show up, and several players walked across the street to the Jack-in-the-Box. The fare at the Ramada Inn was pancakes without syrup and cereal without milk.

During the previous night, Applewhite was suffering from an intestinal virus and was up all night while his roommate Chris Simms slept. Applewhite received IVs before the game, and Simms started the A&M game. Applewhite came in during the third quarter, but could not engineer a victory.

Rematch with Nebraska

Things didn't improve much for the Longhorns a week later when they fell to Nebraska 22-6 in the 1999 Big 12 title game in San Antonio. Against Nebraska, UT's offense failed to score a touchdown for the first time since 1985.

Nebraska allowed just nine yards rushing on 29 carries, the lowest total in UT history until OU allowed UT minus-seven yards rushing in a 63-14 victory over the Longhorns in 2000.

Roy Williams: The Playmaker

During the 2000 season, freshman receiver Roy Williams became UT's biggest target for either Major Applewhite or Chris Simms. The six-foot-five, 210-pound Williams set 13 Texas freshman records and two UT single-game records.

The Odessa, Texas, superstar caught 40 passes for 809 yards and eight touchdowns. He also rushed for two touchdowns.

"Roy's athletic ability in my mind has no equal in college football," UT's sophomore quarterback Chris Simms said. "I try to get him the ball in good spots so he can go and make plays. Whatever the

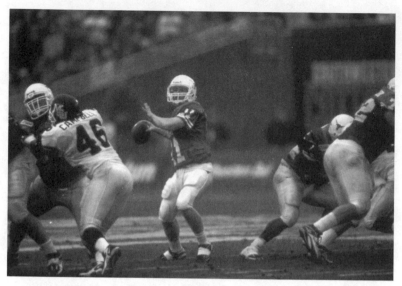

Major Applewhite became a crowd favorite at Texas home games after leading UT to two victories over Nebraska. *Cotton Bowl Athletic Association*

situation, Roy can go one on one with anybody. I can throw it up. And he is six foot five with long arms and can jump out of the stadium.

"His freshman year we were playing Texas A&M and we were backed up on our own two-yard line," Simms recalls of a 43-17 UT victory. "That is not a great place to be, especially against Texas A&M. He ran deep down the field, probably 40 to 45 yards down the left side. He got turned around. He back-pedaled and stuck his hand out and caught it up there with his right hand."

Holiday Bowl Miscues

Texas finished second in the Big 12 South Division in 2000 because it lost to Oklahoma 63-14. The Longhorns dropped only two regular-season games, including a 27-24 loss at Stanford. And they won their last six games heading into a Holiday Bowl date with Oregon.

Texas lost to the Ducks 35-30. But a fourth-quarter drive directed by Chris Simms was stopped short of a winning score when UT receivers dropped several easy passes.

"I can't get it out of my mind," UT receiver Roy Williams said several months later. "Everybody saw what happened. Texas receivers dropped those passes. It is just like Michael Jordan making the last shot. Everybody remembers the last shot. I believe the receiving corps made big plays all year. But all they remember are the drops at the end because they cost us the game. That's fair."

2001 Quarterback Controversy

In a controversial decision in 2001, Simms won the starting quarterback job from Major Applewhite, a senior, and started 12 straight games during that season.

But in the 12th game, Simms self-destructed in the first half of the 2001 Big 12 championship loss to Colorado 39-37. Applewhite relieved Simms in the Big 12 title game and nearly pulled out a victory.

Simms didn't play a down in UT's 47-43 Holiday Bowl victory over Washington. And Applewhite was named the Offensive MVP of the game when he passed for 473 yards and four touchdowns.

"It was a horrible way to end the year," said Simms of his benching for the bowl game. "It is part of playing college football. You are going to have good and bad games. The thing that hurts is I didn't get a chance to rebound. I didn't get a chance to play in the bowl game. I have spent nine months with thoughts about that last game in my mind. And that stinks, being a quarterback."

Tailgating Becomes Fashionable

Before Mack Brown became head coach at Texas in 1998, tailgating wasn't fashionable at games in Austin. But Brown brought a whole new pre- and postgame philosophy to UT.

Longhorn fans used to park themselves on sixth Street and drink margaritas at various bars and show up late for the games.

Brown initiated the slogan "Be Early, Be Loud, Stay Late" to Austin. And the fans began to arrive early for tailgating spots.

Some came as early as the night before to stake out spots for tailgating, including "The Texas Tailgaters," established in 1998. They have the closest spot to Memorial Stadium.

The idea was the brainchild of two former Texas cheerleaders, Tollie Bernard and John Gillis, "20-somethings" who cheered for UT in the early 1990s and now are white-collar professionals in Austin turned burnt orange fanatics on weekends.

"I think before Mack Brown got here there may have been only a couple of tailgates," Gillis said.

"Now they start 12 blocks south of here," Bernard said. "It starts at the capitol."

Gillis and Bernard said Brown loosened the rules for bringing kegs on campus for football games. And thus the good times and suds began to roll at Texas home games.

Under the Oaks

Close by the "Texas Tailgaters" for each home game is another large gathering of Texas Exes, organized in part by Ken Capps of Dallas, UT's Super Fan.

Capps directed the Longhorn Band on Thursday night before the 2002 season opener against North Texas in honor of his birthday.

Capps, who doubles (when he is not cheering for Texas) as public relations director of DFW Airport, also owns the dubious distinction of being the first tailgater to invite the 25-year-old University of Texas Mariachis to serenade a tailgate.

He did it as the start of what he had hoped was "The Tour to Tempe" and a spot in the Fiesta Bowl for the national championship. But the Longhorns had a detour to Dallas and beat LSU in the Cotton Bowl instead.

The UT SID Streak

Longtime UT publicist Bill Little has set the all-time record for consecutive games worked by a Division I-A sports information director. Through the middle of the 2005 season, Little had been present and working at every Longhorn football game since Texas battled Baylor on November 7, 1970.

Under coach Mack Brown, tailgating became popular with the slogan: "Be Early, Be Loud, Stay Late." *Ronald Martinez/Getty Images*

That's a streak of 414 straight games and betters the longest previous streak among Division I-A sports information directors (Syracuse's Larry Kimball, 383).

Little missed the SMU game on October 31, 1970, because his mother passed away right before the game.

Midway through the 2005 season, Little has worked 27 bowl games. But he almost missed the 1995 Nokia Sugar Bowl when Texas lost to Virginia Tech 28-10, because he suffered a heart attack while with the team in New Orleans. But the resourceful Little talked his way out of the hospital.

"The next day I talked to the doctor," Little said. "He told me there had not been that much damage to the artery. I told him I had a really nice suite at the Hilton overlooking the river. He agreed to let me go back there. And once he agreed to that, I asked him if I could go to the game."

Climbing to the Top

Texas coach Mack Brown has lifted the Longhorns to a place among the elite heading into the 2005 season. And Brown, himself, is on a lofty plateau as well.

Only two Division I-A programs have had seven consecutive nine-victory seasons, Texas and Miami, Florida. And Brown is the only active Division I-A coach with a nine-year streak of nine or more victories each season entering the 2005 season.

Brown's active streak of 15 straight winning seasons and 13 consecutive bowl appearances—fashioned at both Texas and North Carolina—is surpassed only by Florida State coach Bobby Bowden's 28 straight winning seasons and 23 straight bowl trips.

Under Brown, Texas has posted seven straight seasons of nine or more victories for the first time in school history

"Mack's like the Darrell Royal of the 21st century," said UT All-America offensive tackle Jerry Sisemore.

CHAPTER THIRTEEN

First Disappointment, Then Elation

Arkansas Shocker and Rebounder

One of two key nonconference games for Texas in the 2003 season was a game in Austin against Arkansas, an old Southwest Conference foe.

It was the first regular-season meeting between the Longhorns and Razorbacks since the Razorbacks left the SWC for the SEC following the 1991 season. The two teams also met in the 2000 Cotton Bowl, with Arkansas winning 27-6.

Prior to the 2003 regular-season game, Arkansas insiders said that Razorbacks coach Houston Nutt had assistants call Oklahoma assistants and find out what their secret for success was against the Longhorns in their annual game in Dallas. They were told by their Sooners counterparts: Be real physical with Texas, and the Longhorns will give up.

The player who may have been the most physical was surprising. Arkansas quarterback Matt Jones rushed for 102 yards on 12 carries and passed for 139 yards and one touchdown. Behind Jones, Arkansas scored 21 straight points in the first half to take control of the game and eventually win 38-28.

In 2004 Texas returned the favor, however, by defeating the Razorbacks 22-20 in Fayetteville and by forcing three Arkansas turnovers in the final 10 minutes of the game, ending the brief two-game series on a high note.

A Call, and Meeting with Knight

Texas Tech coach Bob Knight called Mack Brown after the 2003 loss to Oklahoma and told Brown he was doing a good job. Brown, formerly the North Carolina football coach, knew Knight through North Carolina basketball coaches Dean Smith and Bill Guthridge.

Then before Texas Tech played a basketball game in Austin, Pat Knight, Bob's son and assistant coach, saw Mack Brown out in the hall at the Erwin Center and said, "Dad wants you to come into the locker room and talk to him."

So Brown went to meet Knight, who was sitting in the locker room at the Erwin Center with his shoes off and his feet propped up over two chairs while reading a book. That call and meeting meant a lot to Brown.

Going to the Holiday Bowl—Again

Despite the 2003 loss to Oklahoma, Texas still had a chance to go to a BCS Bowl. That was until the top-ranked Sooners suffered a stunning loss to Kansas State in the Big 12 championship game in Kansas City, Missouri.

Oklahoma's loss allowed the Big 12 champion Wildcats to effectively take UT's place in the Tostitos Fiesta Bowl. The Sooners were an at-large team in the BCS and played LSU for the national championship in the Nokia Sugar Bowl.

Texas slipped to the Holiday Bowl, where the Longhorns lost to Washington State 28-20.

"They beat us once and screwed us twice," Texas coach Mack Brown said of the Sooners. "Sally and I were watching the game and after a little while, she said, 'We are out of here.'"

Brown indicated he knew his team was in trouble going into the 2003 Holiday Bowl, simply because this was the third time in four seasons the Longhorns had wound up in San Diego.

"We had good practices," Brown said. "But two days before the game I knew we were in trouble. The game was going on, but they were looking at their watches, like when are we getting out of here."

Vince Young Coming of Age in 2004

UT quarterback Vince Young can pinpoint the moment he believes he came of age during the 2004 season. Young and Brown had a meeting after the Longhorns defeated Missouri 28-20 in Austin following a 12-0 shutout loss to Oklahoma in Dallas the previous week.

"After the Missouri game, Coach gave me more plays, and the offensive opened up," Young said of when the quarterback competition between himself and Chance Mock ended.

Brown told the six-foot-five, 230-pound Young to be himself and do the things the coaches had seen him do in practice.

Under Young's leadership, Texas came from behind in the second half to win its final four games of the 2004 season, including the Rose Bowl against Michigan. Counting early-game deficits against Texas Tech and Colorado, Young led UT back in the final six games of the 2004 season.

"We kept seeing it," Brown said. "It really came out at Texas Tech. He was the guy we had seen in practice."

Behind Young's 300 yards of total offense, Texas crushed Texas Tech 51-21 in Lubbock as Young started the game. A week later he was instrumental in helping UT score 31 straight points after the first quarter in a 31-7 win at Colorado.

Back in Austin, Young led a 49-straight-point onslaught for a 56-35 victory against Oklahoma State after the Cowboys had taken a 35-7 lead. Young had more than 400 yards total offense against Oklahoma State in UT's biggest comeback in history and would duplicate that the next week against Kansas.

"He is quick, but he has power," Brown said of Young. "The stat we talked to him about was becoming the winningest quarterback in Texas history."

Brown said UT's penchant to come back in 2004 was a combination of several factors.

"In the third and fourth quarters, Cedric [Benson] was so tough," Brown said. "The offensive line was good and would beat them down. And they would get tired of chasing [Young]. He didn't want to come out of the game. And he was in such phenomenal shape."

Last Gasp vs. Kansas

The 10th game of the 2004 season versus Kansas in Lawrence was something special, even for the athletic Young.

Texas trailed the unranked Jayhawks, who had a losing record, 23-13 with less than seven minutes to go. Young brought the Longhorns within three points on a dazzling 18-yard run with 4:12 remaining.

The Longhorns caught a break on a controversial pass interference call on Kansas, which then had to punt. But on the ensuing possession UT appeared to bog down on fourth down, when Young's feet took over.

Young's big run set up his winning touchdown pass of 21 yards to Tony Jeffery with 11 seconds remaining.

"The most phenomenal play," UT coach Mack Brown said of the run. "It was fourth and 18, and Vince ran for 25 yards. After he gained seven yards, he looked downfield as if he was going to pass, I said, 'Oh, no!' I asked him after the game—I knew I would be talking to you guys—'Can we say it was quarterback draw?'"

Brown added, "He said he knew he could make the first down because, 'There was only one guy out in the flat, and he couldn't tackle me.'"

"At that time, I didn't think we would have a fourth-and-18," Young said of the fired-up Jayhawks' defense. "They had two sacks. The fans were coming out [from the basketball lines at Allen Field House as word spread the Jayhawks were beating the Longhorns in a huge upset] and it was getting louder."

Texas A&M Turnaround: Mid-Game

In Game No. 11 of the 2004 season, Texas quarterback Vince Young appeared to the going in for a touchdown right before halftime of the Texas A&M game in Austin. But he fumbled trying to get the ball over the goal line. The Aggies got it and ran it 98 yards for a touchdown. The vast majority of the 85,000 in attendance, except for a small section of the Aggies faithful in the lower bowl in the northwest part of the stadium, were stunned.

For the second straight game, it looked as if UT's BCS hopes were in peril. Texas A&M—not Texas—led 13-6 at halftime.

"There's a 93 percent chance when there is a 14-point swing like that right before halftime, the team [that is behind] will lose," Brown said. "[Vince] wasn't talking much at halftime. In the second half, he took it and just wasn't going to lose the game. He ended up dominating the game. It was not nearly as close as the score indicated."

Texas outscored the Aggies 20-0 in the second half to win 26-13 and finish the regular season 10-1.

Brown the Politician

Unfortunately, UT coach Mack Brown knew UT's bridesmaid's path of 2004 could have been: lose to OU in Dallas, fail to win the Big 12 South, and wind up outside of the Bowl Championship Series once more.

UT players came to Brown the week before the Longhorns' traditional Thanksgiving Week game against Texas A&M.

"They came to me that week and said they were tired of going to the same place—the Holiday Bowl," Brown said. "They wanted to go to Orlando. I told them that it didn't work that way. But I told them if they beat Texas A&M, I would take their case to the media. I did not know it would get as big a play as it did."

Sure enough, Brown got enough human voters to move Texas up in the BCS standings to No. 4 past California so it could make a BCS Bowl as an at-large entry from the Big 12. And the Longhorns wound up going to the Rose Bowl for the first time.

Texas players celebrate the game-winning kick by Dusty Mangum (No. 14), which edged the Wolverines 38-37 in the Rose Bowl. *Donlad Miralle/Getty Images*

Fiesty Fan at the Rose Bowl

Texas had a chance to go the Fiesta Bowl, but because the Longhorns had never played Michigan nor in the Rose Bowl, UT officials elected to go to Pasadena.

A Rose Bowl official, dressed in traditional white coat and white pants was talking to UT fan Barbara Stuart and was complaining of how he longed for the good ol' days when there was always a Big Ten *and* a Pac-10 team playing in Pasadena.

The feisty four-foot-11 Stuart—the wife of former Cotton Bowl president John Stuart, a Texas Ex and a wealthy and influential Dallas banker, said, "Well, we used to always like to go to the Cotton Bowl as SWC champions, but those days are over. Get over it!"

Dusty's Kick Has Little Velocity, But It Was Good Enough

The 2005 Rose Bowl game came down to Dusty Mangum's 37-yard field goal as time expired. It went through the uprights, however wobbly, to give Texas a 38-37 victory in its first game against Michigan.

With two seconds remaining and Texas trailing 37-35, Mangum, a senior, lined up for the final and most important play of his college career. Michigan called two timeouts to try to ice Mangum. And the Wolverines actually may have got a hand on the ball after it was kicked.

"I think it got tipped because it changed the rotation on the ball," Mangum said. "I saw it was still going straight and I knew it was good because it wasn't winding or curving or anything like that. I had an idea it had been touched because the rotation definitely changed on the ball."

Longhorns Answer Critics in Rose Bowl

Pac-10 fans who believed Cal should have been in Pasadena instead of the Longhorns couldn't really make that case when the Golden Bears lost to Texas Tech in the Holiday Bowl and Texas beat Michigan 38-37 in one of the greatest Rose Bowls of all time.

Young put on a tremendous show and certainly labeled himself as a strong challenger for the 2005 Heisman Trophy. Against the Wolverines, he ran for 192 yards and four touchdowns and passed for 180 yards and another score. He had touchdown runs of 20, 50, 10, and 23 yards. Michigan tended to focus on UT running back Cedric Benson, who had 70 yards on 23 carries.

"Michigan does a great job on their assignments," Young said. "They had a spy on Cedric Benson. They were doing a lot of things to stop Cedric. And Cedric had gotten an injury to his leg. Coach told me to take over the game."

"The Rose Bowl has helped Vince's confidence," Brown said. "He is good enough to win the Heisman if he keeps working hard and our team is good. We had to have a good team."

Entering the 2005 Season

Vince Young had the best completion passing rate (59 percent) of any quarterback in UT history after two seasons and also had accounted for more touchdowns (43) and more rushing yards (2,077) in his first two seasons than any previous UT quarterback.

Young said he took his high school press clippings and folded them away after he saw what he was up against at Texas.

"I got hit in the head in practice; I saw all the great players out there," Young said of settling his game down. "I knew I had to calm down, shut my mouth, and learn the game and stay humble."

His mother back in Houston makes sure of that.

"Every morning at five o'clock, my mother calls me and gives me words from The Bible," Young said. "It is a different quote from a scripture. Sometimes I pick up the phone and sometimes I get it off my answering machine."

Beating Ohio State

In the space of three games over two seasons, Texas played two of the most storied programs in college football history—Michigan in the January 1, 2005, Rose Bowl and Ohio State early in the 2005 season.

And with No. 2 UT's 25-22 victory over the No. 4 Buckeyes on September 10 in Columbus, the early-season buzz was Texas very well could be the team that could run the table and play No. 1 USC in the 2006 Rose Bowl for the national championship.

"Coming out of the Rose Bowl, it was so much fun … and it was an exiting game like this one," Texas coach Mack Brown said after the Ohio State victory. "And coming up here, everybody picked us to lose. All the [Longhorns] kids who watch TV said nobody gave us a chance, and you can't win here."

With the victory over Ohio State, Texas ran its streak to 10 straight victories over opponents in their home stadiums. A victory over Missouri on October 1 in Columbia would run Texas's streak to 11.

The Texas victory also ended Ohio State's 36-game nonconference home winning streak and Brown's eight-game losing streak against top 10 teams.

It was a loose Texas team that took the field at Ohio State and pulled out the victory.

"I don't know where it comes from, but everybody says we are uptight," Brown said. "Shoot, they're dancing in the dressing room. If I let you all in there, you wouldn't believe it. In fact, I want to turn down the music sometimes because it's too loud in the locker room."

Young Gets Assists

UT quarterback Vince Young made the plays when he needed to beat Ohio State, attacking the Buckeyes' secondary. His passes to freshman running back Jamaal Charles (six catches, 69 yards) and sophomore receiver Billy Pittman (five catches, 130 yards) were crucial.

Young passed for 270 yards against the Buckeyes. A 24-yard pass to Limas Sweed with 2:37 remaining won the game for the Longhorns.

"I think you have to put people into the box to stop his run," said Ohio State coach Jim Tressel. "And there are times when the pass is going to be a little bit vulnerable.... He's a good football player. He played hard. And you could see he was getting hit and beat up and kept coming back. I just have a lot of respect for him."

Young was at his best near the end of the game when he took Texas on a seven-play 67-yard touchdown drive to win the game with 2:37 remaining.

"It's basically staying poised, man, knowing ... do not turn the ball over, take care of the ball, just find the plays, and take it a play at a time," Young said. "We've got some great athletes on our side of the ball."

Celebrate the Variety of American and Texas Sports
in These Other Releases from Sports Publishing!

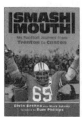

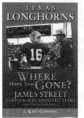